Revolution and Fall

*Christian Life
in a
Post-Christian World*

CHARLES GRICE

authorHOUSE®

AuthorHouse™
1663 Liberty Drive
Bloomington, IN 47403
www.authorhouse.com
Phone: 1 (800) 839-8640

© *2016 charles grice. All rights reserved.*

No part of this book may be reproduced, stored in a retrieval system, or transmitted by any means without the written permission of the author.

Published by AuthorHouse 12/06/2016

ISBN: 978-1-5246-5388-0 (sc)
ISBN: 978-1-5246-5387-3 (e)

Print information available on the last page.

Any people depicted in stock imagery provided by Thinkstock are models, and such images are being used for illustrative purposes only.
Certain stock imagery © Thinkstock.

This book is printed on acid-free paper.

Because of the dynamic nature of the Internet, any web addresses or links contained in this book may have changed since publication and may no longer be valid. The views expressed in this work are solely those of the author and do not necessarily reflect the views of the publisher, and the publisher hereby disclaims any responsibility for them.

The Scripture quotations contained herein are from the New Revised Standard Version Bible, copyright 1989 by the Division of Christian Education of the National Council of Churches of Christ in the U.S.A., and are used by permission. All rights reserved.

Contents

Chapter One: The Revolution 1
Chapter Two: What Do We Mean By Culture? 8
Chapter Three: How the Enlightenment Left Us in the Dark 19
Chapter Four: Out of the Rubble 31
Chapter Five: Secular Humanists: Who Are They? 37
Chapter Six: The Altar of Science 49
Chapter Seven: Messages of Modernity 62
Chapter Eight: Within The Walls 72
Chapter Nine: Ten Questions Christians Must Answer 86
Chapter Ten: The Public Square 99
Chapter Eleven: A Christian Response 113

Chapter One

The Revolution

1 John 4:1 Beloved, do not believe every spirit, but test the spirits to see whether they are from God; for many false prophets have gone out into the world.

This is about the most profound and far-reaching revolution in the history of Western Civilization, a revolution from our Christian foundations to what historians now call a Post-Christian world. No shot was fired, no government was overthrown, no one took to the streets. Yet it was a revolution which, over time, revealed itself to be more sweeping than any other social or political movement in our history. More profound because it represented a revolution in thought, which in turn became a revolution in beliefs which lie at the core of culture, beliefs as to who we are as human, how we should live together and where the future is taking us.

The Post-Christian revolution drew much of its strength from its subtlety, a slow and steady march over centuries, often under the pretext of science or philosophy, carrying the seemingly unassailable banners of freedom, progress or reason. For the most part the Church remained silent. Confronted by the revolution, it engaged in a slow ritualistic form of suicide in its attempt to adapt to this new spirit of the age. Abandoning its roots, it was unable to summon even a word of protest.

The secular movement carried another advantage. It was a message that flattered man. It showed us a new humanity unbound and autonomous, free from all constraints of the past. Much like the serpent's temptation in Genesis, to be like God, Western man ate the fruit and now finds himself in another kind of exile. Alienated from God, we are now alienated from one another and from our best selves. Mired in an age of anxiety and malaise, we are no longer at home in our world.

In Europe the revolution is all but complete. In many of their countries less than ten percent are affiliated with the Church. Here in America the struggle rages on, underlying our deep division. They appear political, but lie much deeper under the surface of things, two groups who can't cooperate, who don't even speak the same language because their differences lie in irreconcilable worldviews.

I saw for myself the statistics of Europe while visiting the great cathedrals of London, Milan, Paris and Rome. In Milan during a worship service, I sat alone in my pew, with only a few elderly scattered about a massive sanctuary that once held thousands. Later in the day I returned when the cathedral was open to the public. The noise of tourists milling about, eating and taking pictures as they pointed at the sculptures and architecture, spoke of a curiosity without a history, having no sense of reverence for place. They gazed at the highest expressions of European art, unaware of the artists' faith. They admired the high majestic arches and stained glass windows, with little understanding of the builders' devotion, the centuries-long commitment of generations in its making. Filled with tourists, it was emptied of its spirit.

Some will say this isn't all that revolutionary, just part of the inevitable ebb and flow of history. Rather than offering dozens of anecdotes as a counterpoint, such as activist courts upending long standing traditions or bestselling books written by militant atheists, I offer a brief thought experiment.

Let's extract three couples from three different eras and place them into our century. One from Europe's Middle Ages, one from the United States Revolutionary War period and a third from the recent past, an American couple just after World War II. When we insert them into today's world, our initial thoughts are directed towards a different revolution, one I don't consider all that revolutionary. We'd want to know how they would react to our technology, everything from smart phones to jumbo jets. Those things would dazzle, but only for a while. Over time our modern inventions would lose their magic. The real revolution lies underneath and can be unearthed by asking them a few questions.

Do you believe you possess a soul? Implicit in this question is a challenge to a modern view of humanity as highly evolved organisms defined only by our chemistry and biology. A second question, do you believe in an entity we can call evil? This is another challenge to today's thinking, evil as the stuff of myth and superstition, along with the modern claim that our problems are the effects of oppressive social structures. This of course reflects modernity's own mythmaking, a belief in the eventual perfection of man by man. If we only refine our methods of social engineering, enhance our sensitivity training, if we fund enough programs and ride the wave of technology, a grand new world will soon emerge. This is the secular experiment we've been living in for decades. When faced with its self-evident failures, modernity reaches into its bottomless bag of still more utopian promises, just more finely-tuned social engineering and more training, unable to see that our problems are human problems, not the problems of biological accidents. Related to the question of evil is the question of sin, a word now erased from the public square. The post-revolutionary man is free to define herself or himself on their own terms. Free from God, who can we sin against?

The power and reach of our Post-Christian transformation is revealed by the answers these three couples would give. Do you have a soul? "Of course," they'd answer, likely wondering why you asked. Theirs is a Christian answer, once the bedrock of Western civilization, with the soul as the most basic assumption of our self-identity. We are made in the image of God.

Is there such a thing as evil and sin? All of them would reply with an emphatic yes, not with abstract sociological responses. They could give you examples of our human history of war and strife. On a personal level, they would acknowledge themselves as fallen; still another reflection of the once Christian worldview that man is unable to save man.

Their answers would contain such phrases as "that's how things are," or "everyone thinks that way," evidence of what we call culture, something we will explore in the next chapter. But the radical reach of the revolution is revealed not just in their answers. It is revealed by the fact that these couples, whose different lives span over a thousand years, would all give you much the same answers. Fixed in a Judeo-Christian mindset, they would share the same outlook upon life, the same view of themselves, ideas fixed and stable as cultural assumptions, until now.

The following chapters are an attempt to understand how and why we find ourselves in this Post-Christian world. Only when we're able to understand the how and why, as well as the revolution's means of persuasion, can Christians begin to form a proper response and regain their confidence.

On several occasions I've presented this topic to various groups under the title of 'Christianity and Culture: Are We at War?' Usually as I'm gathering my notes after a presentation, there's a line at the podium, people wanting to know more. More or less they have the same question one woman asked, her voice displaying deep distress, "What can we do?" That is what this book is about, what we can do, the question which lies at the heart of Christian discipleship. Faced with our new world, I find Christians either in a state of denial and withdrawal, or reduced to angry hand-wringing. These attitudes not only betray the assurances given to Christians, a world still in God's hands, but they also betray our great commission, to go out and to love a lost world. But before we can speak this Christian truth to our world, we must first understand the lie it is living.

Chapter Two is entitled, "What Do We Mean by Culture?" If we want to understand this seismic shift of the West, first we need to know something about culture itself, its foundations and how it works. In using the term Western culture, I'm referring to the civilization arising out of the ashes of Rome, migrating north from the Mediterranean throughout the European continent, later imported to the new world. Today we can't envision how thoroughly Christianity once pervaded the West, not just one influence among many, but an embedded worldview which formed a distinct culture. Faith transcended nationality. Kings and queens sought the authority of the Church for their legitimacy. At the center of almost all old European cities there stood a church. The disciplines of their early universities, science, philosophy, astronomy and mathematics were all taught in the service of theology. Art and literature, from Michelangelo to Milton, were anchored in the expression of Christian faith.

Chapter Three, "How the Enlightenment Left Us In the Dark," looks back to the seeds of thought which eventually gave rise to today's Post-Christian culture. Historians generally agree that it was the philosophy of the Enlightenment beginning in 16th Century Europe, which eventually shaped the mindset of the secular world as we now know it. By tracing the development of ideas from the Enlightenment, we will not only gain an understanding as to how it was able to undermine Christianity, but we'll see its inherent flaws and weaknesses.

Chapter Four, "Out of the Rubble," revisits the collapse of the Enlightenment project in the aftermath of two World Wars. With millions lying dead on the battlefield, Europe was forced to look in the mirror. Here we will examine the choices it made, choices which are still with us today.

Chapter Five studies "Secular Humanism" asking what is it and what are its beliefs? The term 'secular' means those areas of life, such as government or business, in which religious influence is generally absent. When the term secular is joined with the term 'humanism,' as it is today, it embodies a comprehensive belief system more prevalent than many realize.

Chapter Six, entitled "Altar of Science," doesn't engage in the tiresome and unnecessary debate as to whether science and religion can coexist. The history of the West, other than a few isolated incidents, was not only one where faith and scientific inquiry got along, but one of mutual encouragement. Isaac Newton, Albert Einstein and a long list of Nobel Prize winners were all persons of faith. This chapter is about something else, a distortion of science I call pseudoscience which doesn't limit itself to the scientific method, hijacking real science to make philosophical or quasi-religious claims. Since this is one of the agnostic world's most powerful tools of persuasion, we need to understand its agenda.

Chapter Seven, "Within the Walls," looks at the way secularism, with its activist bent, undermines the traditions and beliefs of the Church. Here we will take a look at two of their assaults upon Christianity, one upon its creeds and another under the pretext of social justice.

Chapter Eight, "Messages of Modernity," asks several questions of today's culture which should be an embarrassment to modernity. Questions it cannot answer. What happened to the greatness of Western art, literature and classical music? Where are today's creative geniuses who can rival Shakespeare, Rembrandt or Mozart? Is the abandonment of Western classical studies by our universities a reflection of this embarrassment, or is it a repudiation of our past so that it can install a culture of its own?

Chapter Nine presents "Ten Questions Christians Must Answer." Only a few decades ago these questions would never have been posed to the Christian faith. In a once stable culture of shared values and meaning, these answers were considered settled. A Post-Christian world now questions faith in the spirit of antagonism rather than inquiry. Christians need to know how to answer, and in knowing what we believe, we will reclaim our confidence, realizing that faith does in fact provide life's compelling answers.

Chapter Ten takes a look at the "Public Square" and its history in America, asking how our historical dialogue, which used to talk about shared values and the common good, has turned into today's shrill and toxic shouting match over rights and power, no longer seeking truths by which a nation can live.

In the final chapter, "A Christian Response," I return to the question of what we can do. The hope is that these chapters, by giving the reader an understanding of how this secular revolution began, as well as its methods and its underlying beliefs, we will then know what to do. We will see how tenuous are the foundations of this revolution, and how it is beginning to sow the seeds of its own demise. Yet much like the early disciples, first we must be equipped and prepared before we can go out into our world.

I write from a Christian perspective. I can write from no other. One of the modern lies we've been handed is that faith can be reduced to our personal preferences. With seemingly unassailable words like 'choice' tossed about, we're confused about something. We're confused about truth. Of course we're free to choose our own belief system, but in today's individualized world, we've stopped asking of things, "Is this really true? And if this is really true, is it not true for everyone?" Every religious tradition once directed a person towards this one idea, a belief in something absolute and timeless, a reality beyond us rather than the subjective. Faith had to do with the nature of man and the nature of God, and within such truths our destiny rather than our own projections. So complete is the revolution, such questions have given way to vague notions of tolerance and inclusivity, with any absolute claims subject to derision, except of course the absolutism of their Post-Christian claims. In a world we did not make, a life we didn't create, standing in a universe we cannot comprehend, the human predicament has somehow become a self-construction. In taking our first step, as we try to understand this strange new world in which we find ourselves, we need to ask and answer an initial question. What is culture?

Chapter Two

What Do We Mean By Culture?

2 Timothy 4:3 For the time is coming when people will not put up with sound doctrine, but having itching ears, they will accumulate for themselves teachers to suit their own desires, and will turn away from listening to truth and wander away to myths.

If we want to understand how our culture has changed, we must first understand culture, what it is and how it exerts its influence. A definition is elusive. We're so immersed in our own culture, for the most part we're unaware of its workings. Trying to explain it to someone is much like telling a fish it's wet. Still, we can venture some thoughts. One is by way of comparison, looking back at old cultural foundations which once held firm in the West but no longer bind us.

Culture is not to be confused with civilization. A nation can be civilized, possessing advanced technology, yet with very different ideas about democracy, the role of women, the rites of childhood or even the worth of the individual. Culture binds us subtly and powerfully, with its traditions constantly enacted and reenacted in order to reinforce itself. In this manner culture transmits its own set of values and virtues, providing nothing less than a comprehensive outlook upon life. Strong culture is like the air we breathe, invisible, yet life sustaining.

Likely culture arose initially from the need for survival, binding people against external threats. At first this took the form of military or economic ties rather than sharing a common spirit. Ancient Rome is referred to as an empire, not a culture, because it was held together primarily by military might, ultimately proving to be a weak union. Once the Roman projection of power waned, its fracture was swift and inevitable. Rising from the collapse, a different type of conquest took place, this one spiritual. Christianity quickly spread from its Mediterranean roots, sweeping across Europe, holding it together somewhat loosely through the Dark Ages. Over time it became a strong culture by providing more than protection or economic benefit. More than that, it provided a spiritual framework for both the community and the individual. Unlike primitive or weak cultures, Christianity was able to supply answers for living as well as answers for dying.

Christianity became so imbedded in the European psyche, so widely shared in its way of thinking, we were the fish unaware of the water in which we were swimming. All cultures to a different degree, give something tangible to its people in the form of answers to our basic human questions, ones we are born with. Usually these take four basic forms: Where did everything come from? Who am I and how do I fit within this creation? What constitutes living a good life? Finally the question of death, where is everything going?

Because each of the four questions is related to the other, we will take the first two together. How did the world come about and who am I within it? Every culture has provided some sort of answer. Each had its own creation story. Some of the early answers, although partial, arose from primitive animist beliefs, which believed in a preexisting eternal cosmos of which the earth was at the center. It was a reality we could not peer beyond. This gave the earth a form of eternal permanence since it alone appeared unchanging while yielding plants and animals who came and went. Generations passed but only the earth remained. Possessing this life-giving magic, the world itself was the object of worship as early man simply considered himself to be a part of nature, caught up in the same cycle as the plants and animals. It was a weak transmission of culture, man was not unique, with questions of life and death yielding little. It was a diminished hope if anything, humans like the harvest, flourished in their spring and summer, followed by an eventual winter.

The Pre-Socratic Greeks attempted to go further, positing an explanation of human beginnings in the hope we were somehow unique. They speculated that man emerged from elemental forces, some said water, while others claimed fire or air. This still left us to wonder, where did these forces come from? Did it really say who I am? Because man remained soulless, culture remained both primitive and weak, binding us loosely. Several centuries later, one of the pillars of Western culture arose in the form of classical Greek philosophy, in particular Plato and his philosophy of the Logos. He claimed there was something beyond it all, beyond the elements in the form of a pure and eternal consciousness from which all things came about. His Logos was the highest of all realities, but for the Platonists as each reality proceeded from the Logos, in succession that wave of creation created the next wave of reality until the earth and man were eventually formed. According to the Stoics, this succession of creative acts distanced us from the perfect Logos, making our world and our bodies something base and corrupt. For the Platonist the goal was an escape from the physical through the attainment of wisdom. This distance of humanity from an impersonal Logos made for a remote god. Answers remained partial. Western culture had taken a step forward in providing some of life's answers, but not a decisive step.

The West discovered its foundational answers by way of the Judeo-Christian faith. Creation, and the individual's place in creation, came from the story of Genesis, later heightened in the life of Christ. The Genesis narrative was unique, revolutionary to man's thought process. It ventured beyond the elements of nature, beyond our philosophical musings with the words "In the beginning." Genesis told a story of a God beyond time and space, allowing human imagination and belief to soar to new heights. Men and women were no longer set adrift in an impersonal world. This God, absolute and infinite, was paradoxically personal, even though we couldn't completely grasp this paradox. This personal God had a deep and abiding concern for us, infusing the Western mind with new meaning and hope. We were unique, set apart from nature and its inexorable cycle of life and death. Even more, we were loved. Suddenly we were at home in our world.

The West's conception of human nature was found in Genesis' second claim, almost as radical as the claim of an infinite personal God. We were made in his image. In time this became Western culture's unique view of humanity. Our identity, as well as our orientation towards our neighbor, all originated from this Genesis image. Each of us was fashioned in an act of love as God declared on the sixth day of creation, "It is very good." Counterintuitive to all prior human thought and belief, this transcendent God made a decision, his choice to be immanent. He wanted to be in relation with us. He spoke, he revealed himself and he made covenants with us. This supplied the answer to our second fundamental question, "Who am I?" We were not accidents. We weren't subject to the whim of capricious gods. This provided not only the makings of a strong culture but eventually it cultivated a deep respect for life. Over time it engendered a culture of charity and compassion previously unknown in other civilizations. Unlike some Eastern cultures where the individual was subordinate to the collective, Western thought saw the individual as possessing ultimate worth simply because God said so.

With the Western vision of humanity elevated, it was taken to even greater heights by way of the Gospels. This God became incarnate. Man and woman, even in their fallen states, were forever affirmed because God himself had become flesh. Even when Western culture wandered far from its Judeo-Christian morality and ethic, whether it was war or oppression, Christianity always provided the way back. It was our means of constant cultural reform, taking many paths such as the first of the world's democracies or the initial voice for human rights.

The next step for a culture is to provide a framework for how we should live together. This is the third question, what constitutes living a full life? For the Far East, Confucianism regulated the workings of a civil and ordered community. In other cultures, tribal norms were passed down orally. For the West, the Biblical narrative once again provided our framework. Israel, in its Exodus from Egypt, was our first paradigm for nation and community. They represented a free people, with only one ultimate authority in God. We were free from the whims of kings and impersonal gods. Unlike Egypt, Israel would never accept a pharaoh's decree to throw babies in the Nile. In time this vision of freedom and the worth of the individual allowed the West to be the first culture to throw off the yoke of kings, to oppose slavery and to enact laws which protected the individual against the state.

But our concept of freedom wasn't unrestrained. To sustain itself a culture requires boundaries, limits upon the individual which hold back the ever-present threat of chaos. Once again our guide for such order was to be found in Old Testament, in the form of Ten Commandments, given by God only after Israel had formed a nation. The Commandments not only addressed worship and our relationship with God, but also the questions as to how we should live together. They took the form of restraints against individualism by way of 'thou shalt not' commandments, placing limits upon the inclinations of human nature. By honoring father and mother it preserved the family as the basic cultural building block. By prohibiting stealing it protected property. It guarded life by forbidding murder. It addressed the inevitable economic inequalities which arise in any society, forbidding covetousness. Our freedom needed structure. The law needed love and love need the law.

These foundations once constituted a safeguard against the today's rampant individualism. Traditions of the West were once rooted in God's rules, not our own. The modern assault upon religion, with its particular animosity directed towards the Ten Commandments, is in part this struggle of the supreme individual against any outside authority, the clash of absolute freedom versus order.

The idea of a full life found its ultimate expression in the Gospels. Christ was not only fully divine but also fully man. He revealed who God is while at the same time also revealing what it means to be human. This would become the Western model for the good and virtuous life. Did Western man faithfully adhere to this model? Of course not. No culture lives up to its highest principles. Western Culture compromised religion, it abused the rights of individuals, while democracies often forgot their democratic values. But strong culture serves as a compass. In our excesses, it pulls us back towards these enduring truths. In cycles or in times of crisis, it calls us back to reform. There can be no such thing as reform unless there are normative values and fixed truths to which we can return. Rather than the heroes of the secular revolution, Darwin, Nietzsche or Marx, Western man was enjoined to be Christ-like, one who is self-giving and who worships.

Adding to the force and stability of our culture was the fact that these Commandments and our paradigm of Christ were not self-generated. They didn't spring from philosophy, from political necessities or by rulers. They were God given, making them immutable and unquestioned, not subject to shifting standards of time, place and circumstance. None of these answers will provide us with meaning and purpose unless there is an answer to the final question, where is everything going? The question of death lies at the heart of all human yearning and anxiety. If everything in time returns to oblivion, which is today's secular view though repackaged in less stark terms, nothing else matters. Pagan stories attempted to lessen the fear by way of heroic myths, whether the epic poem of Gilgamesh as the demigod protector of the Sumerians or the Greek Odysseus who journeyed to a dark world only to return. In these weak transmissions of culture, the heroic figure faced death, even defied it, but in the end such stories couldn't rescue us. Much like the pagans, the heroic myth has returned in today's proliferation of fantasy and apocalyptic stories. Both modern in their presentation and primitive in their thought, they are a weak form of cultural avoidance.

A culture unable to answer the question of death, cannot ask anything of its people. It cannot ask for sacrifice. It can't ask a generation to build something which will be realized only by another. Our current politics is evidence of a self-indulgent culture, only granting for ourselves benefits in the here and now.

For the West, the question of death was answered in the central claim of Christianity, the resurrection. God's triumph of life over death gave us a unique energy and dynamism. Optimism and hope overcame all obstacles. It meant history was going somewhere, not a random series of events. Historians point to an early period of American history soon after its founding, with an explosion of universities, schools, hospitals and other charitable institutions. Sunday school, for example, was founded by the Church for basic reading and writing in the absence of universal education. The Church and Christianity were at the forefront of these thousands of initiatives, as historians have also written of the motivation of their founders. They believed they were laying the foundations for a future kingdom of God. This is one of the many ironies of today, institutions such as universities attempting to distance themselves from religion, yet standing on its shoulders for their existence.

The Post-Christian world finds itself unable to provide answers to these basic human questions. Where did we come from? You may get a vague reply on a college campus such as the Big Bang which only kicks the can down the road. Who am I? Once you sweep aside their rhetoric, modernity says we're random acts of nature. What is the good life? This used to be a shared answer, now one subjective, answered by each person on their own terms. It's lightly propped up with facile slogans such as 'seize the day' or 'live life to the fullest,' without any content concerning what we are supposed to seize or what may constitutes fullness. Where are we going? What happens at death? They have no answers, underlying today's deep anxiety and unease. Not only are we devoid of answers, but we've stopped asking, abandoning the once supreme pursuit of cultures, not only in the religious realm but the artistic and poetic as well, revealing how much we've lost in this revolution.

The Post-Christian world senses its vulnerability. Instinctively it knows its bankruptcy of meaning. Increasingly unable to compensate with its catchphrases or empty sentimentality, it has begun to resort to its only available method, tearing down. This lies at the heart of the relentless secular agenda in its attempt to push religion to the margins while at the same time rewriting Western history to suit its agenda. All accomplishments of the West must be brought down without balance or objectivity, as secularism can only point to its worst examples, whether religious conflict, colonialism, wars or slavery. Can anything survive the critique of its worst examples? But is this really a critique of Western culture? Was slavery not once universal? Is not all human history one of war? Are there not religious conflicts in every corner of the world, usually with its ends more about power and wealth than religion? The secular criticism of the West is for the most part a sleight of hand, a denunciation of the West aimed at seizing the old bastions of power, rather than a sober assessment of man's shared human history. What can we commend of the West and its Christian roots? At the very least we held a compass, something we are now without.

Still, What is Culture?

Now that we've examined some of the foundations of culture, we can venture a definition of sorts. By supplying these over-arching narratives for life, culture allows us to feel at home in our world. In its most wide-ranging form, it does so by providing a shared moral force as to what is good and bad, sacred or profane, right from wrong. To the modern mind with its concept of weak culture, any shared force is considered a restraint upon the individual, yet secularism, in its pretense of unbridled freedom, quietly substitutes its own moral force whether in the form of campus shaming, its aggrieved righteousness, boycotts and a growing list of do's and don'ts which belie its controlling nature. Lacking answers, its moral force lacks any form of coherence, leaving us mired in our present fractured and unstable world. It has no language to address the common good. The concept of family is whatever we want it to be. Drug use is an individual choice, unmoored from the consideration of any human cost. Living in an epidemic of addiction, suicide and depression, we're just now beginning to ask, what kind of freedom is this?

This shared moral force requires a mechanism in order to sustain itself. Traditionally religion has been the strongest and most enduring means. Family, community and school also provide a moral force. But there are other far more subtle ways in which culture transmits itself. Here we will briefly talk about three of them in the form of ritual, story and institutions.

Ritual is a tangible way of binding us to our past, making life stable and predictable. Ritual also asks for commitment, usually a shared commitment. We enact them in the form of communion, weddings, the pledge of allegiance, national holidays and hundreds of other ways. The Christian creeds are the most enduring, where we stand together and say "I believe," statements about life and death shared with people who lived a thousand years ago. In this way ritual becomes a bulwark against rampant individualism. There are no personal rituals. That's why secularism subjects rituals to its withering scrutiny. Church needs to be updated and get with the times. Religious dogma is under suspicion. The Pledge of Allegiance and the American flag are somehow battlefronts. We think nothing of making up our own wedding vows, dismissive of liturgy passed down for centuries.

Stories are another powerful means of cultural formation. Stories of the past vividly inform the present, as we once looked to the lives of Lincoln, Washington or Joan of Arc as models for our own lives. Through their stories we carried forward virtues such as faith, courage or sacrifice. We wanted to become these great women and men, but modernity opposes the passing down of stories. Heroes of our past must be brought down if they don't achieve our self-perceived modern perfection. How they could have escaped the milieu of their own time, is left unsaid. Story is now replaced with the odd declarations of "this is my story" or "this is my truth," expressions of a weak culture with millions of unconnected stories instilling us with nothing other than reflections of our own personal experiences. In one attempt to rewrite history, a state board of education voted to take out of all textbooks any religious references in the Thanksgiving story. To whom were these Pilgrims giving thanks?

Institutions are another enduring cultural mechanism. Government, court systems, universities, the Church and others have an ethos of their own which both transmits and reflects culture. Since they are traditionally slow to change, institutions once constituted a safeguard against sudden social upheaval. Modernity has its sights set upon institutions as well. Courts declare themselves free from precedent. Government leaders exercise their power without regard for the deliberative process of checks and balances. Rule of law is subordinated to public opinion. Universities have abandoned the study of the Western classics, replacing it with courses reflecting current social trends. Even the small local institutions, from parent teacher organizations to civic clubs, are fading away. They too served a similar function, and in some ways even more tangible because we participated in them, giving us a small stake in how our world was run. In our institutional demise, modernity substitutes an impersonal and ever growing value-neutral government, incapable of picking up the pieces.

The Force

There are hundreds, if not thousands, of ways in which this moral force is carried out. I thought about this after speaking to a young woman who was taking care of the break room at our office. I noticed she was pregnant, and since her mother was an old acquaintance, I walked down the hallway to ask an assistant about her pregnancy. The assistant told me this would be the woman's second child, adding that they shared the same father, also adding that they had made a decision not to get married. I thought to myself that this concept of 'choice' has become almost sacred, overriding all else, including any choice of the child or the concerns of society. It reigned over any moral reflection. I recalled those times in the early 1960s when a woman had a child out of wedlock. Then it was kept quiet, the mother isolated. Such shaming either explicit or implicit, was wrong, but for all its faults it was a cultural mechanism which possessed some utility. At the very least it was a silent advocate for the child. The force, with all its drawbacks, was a force for stability. It represented something more than the supreme individual.

Modernity claims any such force to be an undue restraint. But its opposition is only directed towards the traditions it opposes. Modernity has its own force, its own methods of shaming and isolation, just different rules. At least the old force provided some answers. Still, it wasn't the pregnant woman's choice to remain single which struck me the most. It was the response of the assistant. Her explanation had all the gravity of making lunch plans that day. It was in effect, accepted, the way things were. This to me was the real indicia of the extent of the revolution's triumph. Now we will turn to the next critical question. How did this silent revolution begin?

Chapter Three

How the Enlightenment Left Us in the Dark

Colossians 2:8 See to it that no one takes you captive through philosophy and empty deceit, according to human tradition, according to the elemental spirits of the universe, and not according to Christ.

If Christians want to understand our Post-Christian world, we need to understand its underpinnings and how it began. Once we peer deeper into its belief system, we will then understand how fragile its foundations are.

All great movements of history, whether social or political, require something of the transcendent. If not religious, they draw upon quasi-religious philosophies or utopian claims as their driving force. Masses won't rise up and follow reasoned arguments. The French Revolution wasn't only about the toppling of royalty. Its mottos of a new man and a new world were supplied by Rousseau. The assembled German masses, entranced by the Nazi torchlight, never saw themselves as murderers. The summons was veiled in a new and better world, of a pure Aryan race with Nietzsche providing its philosophical support. People won't take a bold step out of their ordinary lives, for war or revolution, unless they are shown another life, one glorious. Were it not transcendence they were selling, why would the French Revolution, Nazism and the Soviet Union all turn their sights upon the Church? Why the sacking of sanctuaries and the imprisonment of priests when the Church possesses no earthly power to resist? Intuitively all of them knew their utopian message couldn't stand next to the transcendence of the Gospel. For its message to survive, the Church had to be silenced.

Most historians agree that the ideas which eventually gave rise to the Post-Christian revolution had their roots in the Enlightenment, a movement which we will see, extended far beyond its philosophical beginnings. The impact of philosophy may not sound persuasive in our time. We can't name a contemporary philosopher with any influence today, while academia has long since relegated their philosophy departments to distant hallways. But in Sixteenth Century Europe, it held great sway, rivaled only by the Church. Even if the common man or woman on the street wasn't conversant in the latest philosophical trends, their leaders trained by the university, often were. If you're still skeptical of the power of philosophy, consider the fact that Karl Marx never organized one worker, never participated in one political rally, yet Communism which once engulfed half the world, began with a stack of papers scattered about his dining room table.

It was Renee Descartes (1596-1650) who set the Enlightenment on its initial course with his famous words, "I think therefore I am." Philosophers like to consider themselves as innovators, pioneers of new ways of thinking, but most of the time they're attempting to make sense of changes already going around them. Such was the case with the Enlightenment as Sixteenth Century Europe was beginning to emerge from the Middle Ages. The power of the feudal states was giving way to nations and new freedoms. A merchant class was growing in power and influence. The exploration and colonization of the new world expanded the horizon of continental thinking, while at the same time the feuds of the Church and religious wars following the Reformation, left it vulnerable as a source of authority.

Perhaps the greatest influence upon the Enlightenment was science. The Copernican revolution, advanced further by Johannes Kepler, was later followed by an existential jolt in the form of Isaac Newton. With his theories of gravity and motion, armed with power of his calculus, the movement of all things from celestial bodies to the mechanical world could be predicted and explained. The shock may not have been so great had the Catholic Church not fused some of its theology with classical philosophy. Through Thomas Aquinas, the father of Catholic education, the Church married itself to a measure of Aristotle. In ancient Greece philosophy and science worked hand in hand, with Aristotle's theory of motion positing four causes behind the movement of all things, from ships to the planets. There was some rudimentary science in his theory, but his final cause was purely metaphysical. For Aristotle it wasn't something mechanical or mathematical, it was the object's inherent purpose and its essence of being. This final cause was easily adapted to Church doctrine. All it had to do was simply substitute the hand of God behind all things.

Because the Catholic Church had tied a portion of its doctrine to Aristotle, Newton's discoveries had the unintended effect of undermining Church teaching. No longer was the hand of God behind the stars and the planets. He wasn't necessary for an explanation of the mysteries of the cosmos. It could be described mathematically. Newton, a devout Christian, didn't quite see it as all math, writing in his famous treatise Principia, "The most beautiful system of sun, planet and comets could only proceed from the counsel and dominion of an intelligent and perfect being." But others saw it differently. Newton still saw the hand of God, but with his laws of motion, a new way of thinking would now be set in motion.

Prior to the Enlightenment, European philosophy had confined itself to either the religious or metaphysical realms, with little concern for science. But with new explanations of what was once thought mysterious or unknowable, philosophy had to take notice. If they were to explore the depths of reality, philosophers had to deal with science. It was in this context Renee Descartes began his project. He believed man needed an alternative path to God, one which didn't rest on faith alone, as Descartes' new way would become the great watchword of the Enlightenment, reason.

His first step was a radical departure from all prior philosophical methods. Rather than surveying the world around him, he plunged inward with extreme doubt. Since science was able to provide indisputable knowledge, Descartes was looking for the same kind of unassailable knowledge in philosophy. With his inward turn he asked, how can I be certain that I know what I think I know? He questioned everything, even the reality of the world around him. What if I'm living in a dream? What if reality is being distorted by some evil deceiver? As we will see, over time bizarre assumptions lead to equally bizarre conclusions.

Absorbed in his radical doubt, Descartes stumbled upon his ah-ha moment. Even if he couldn't trust his perceptions, there was one thing of which he was sure. He was thinking. This gave us the Enlightenment's opening line, "I think therefore I am," unleashing a new way of thinking and a new way of perceiving our world. According to Descartes, there was only one reliable source of knowledge, our own minds. Knowledge therefore became subjective and individualized, something we will see later achieving its full expression in the form of postmodern relativism. With man now defining and shaping his own world on his own terms, the claims of the Church based upon revelation, of a God who discloses himself, was under assault. In time the Enlightenment would no longer be able to hear the voice of God.

In his quest to find a new way towards God by way of rationality alone, Descartes didn't understand the vast and unbridgeable distance between philosophy and faith. The Judeo-Christian faith never rested upon philosophical foundations. It cannot be known in principle. Its content and reality are embodied in a personal God, whereas philosophy reduces him to impersonal abstractions, ideas confined only to the intellect. Abstractions place an inevitable distance between us and God, who can only be known relationally. Only in fellowship can we ever hear him.

Descartes' human centric philosophy had another impact upon Western thought. If each of us is the ultimate judge of our surroundings, then the individual was also the judge of all prior traditions. With knowledge confined to one's head, one cannot fully engage with or accept the accumulated knowledge of history.

Wisdom lies in our inner voice, rather than wisdom passed down to us by prior generations. This begs the question as to whether strong culture can exist without deep ties to prior beliefs, its institutions and to its legacy of art and literature. In his Discourse on Method, Descartes expressed this new suspicion of the past, "I essentially abandoned the study of letters and resolved to no longer seek any other science than the knowledge of myself," calling his mind "the great book of the world." Cast off from tradition, especially that of the Church, modern man was about to begin his own personal journey, unaccompanied.

There were of course benefits to the Enlightenment. Its appeal to reason dispelled superstition, including a few advanced by the Church. The call to reason also gave space for academic and scientific pursuits free from theological constraints. But the self-absorbed appeal to reason as our only guide had a dark side which would eventually reveal itself. By the very nature of the Enlightenment, with our own minds as the ultimate judge of all things, it lacked the ability to question itself. No longer would Western civilization look into the night sky and see mystery. Armed with reason, we would soon declare ourselves its master.

With the maxim of human reason and tradition cast aside, the Enlightenment lost sight of the questions previously asked by Christianity, Judaism and classical Greek philosophy. What is the nature of man? What is the nature of God? Where is the future taking us? These past traditions also saw man as capable of great heights, but they gave us balance. We were fallen and flawed. The vanity of the Enlightenment only saw the heights, unable to see any limits upon human reason. It didn't take into account our history of constant war and cruelty, presenting us with a hypothetical man who transcended history, rather than man himself. This new man, now cut off from the self-reflection which religion and classical philosophy once urged upon us, was blind to our irrational side. Descartes gave expression to this hubris, "How then is perfection to be sought? Wherein lies our hope? In education and nothing else." Alone, man would begin this experiment of perfecting man.

Emmanuel Kant (1724-1804) took the Enlightenment to even greater heights, becoming its most famous of all philosophers. Like Descartes, Kant was a Christian, yet unable to see the influence his philosophy would have upon orthodox Christianity. With this new emerging man of reason, he too regarded the wisdom of the past with contempt. Writing after the Newtonian revolution, Kant believed even more deeply that philosophy should be confined to the boundaries now set by science. In this manner Kantian philosophy attempted to restrict itself to the natural and observable world, without flights into the metaphysical. To his credit, Kant believed reason had limits. Whenever reason tried to apprehend the transcendent, he said, it broke down and lost its bearings. Because we couldn't apprehend God with our minds, Kant believed the Church, prayer and priests to be useless. But, if man was limited only to reason and only to the observable world, how can we know there is a God? This became the central question for Kant.

Confined to pure reason, God appeared to be inaccessible. Faced with this dilemma, Kant took one of the most significant steps in all of Western philosophy. He reinvented knowledge itself. At the time Kant was also confronted by a group of thinkers calling themselves empiricists. Even more wed to science, these empiricists claimed we couldn't say anything whatsoever about the spiritual or metaphysical world. We could only make statements concerning things we could see and test. Kant realized this as a threat that could lead to the extinction of both religion and philosophy. If we were to believe the empiricists, theologians and philosophers had nothing left to say.

This was the context in which Kant posited what he called his 'organizing principle.' He claimed that our minds are not passive recipients of the outside world, instead they actively organize and interpret our surroundings. How this conclusion remained in the confines of reason and science was left vague. Armed with his organizing principle, Kant would take us even farther down the road of Descartes' subjectivity. According to Kant, the things around us only possessed the reality we gave them. We interpreted and defined the world on our own terms. In the face of the empiricists, this new principle gave Kant the space to say something about the world and its meaning. With humans as the grand interpreter of all things, all the old externals of Western civilization were now ripe for reevaluation or rejection. Not just the physical world, but matters such as morality, virtue and belief would all soon be up for grabs. The Christian foundation of our knowledge of God, in the form of revelation, was finally tossed aside. Jesus' words to Peter following his confession of Christ, "Flesh and blood has not revealed this to you but my Father in heaven," no longer held.

Still, if we are confined to our own minds and without access to the transcendent, where is God to be found in Kant's thinking? He needed to find something in the natural and observable world, which would become his next epiphany. His answer came in the form of his theory of 'natural law.' Kant claimed there was something we could all objectively discern, a universal ethic and morality which all humanity shared. In asking "Where did this law come from?" Kant found his God. For him it was empirically observable in this universal law, revealed in the ways of man. Faith now had no source, no voice, other than us, as Kant's methods revealed the separate and unbridgeable realms of philosophy and faith. The philosopher can comprehend a universe and he can even conjecture a creator of the universe, but only the believer who is open to something outside himself, who sees a Person, can ever hear him speak. Philosophy possesses the capacity to entertain abstract principles, but in the end we can't live by them, nor can we ever love by them.

Natural law is obviously beset with deep problems. It left no room for an incarnate Christ. This new Enlightenment god, who is to be found only in the ways of mankind, is at best a distant god. How can we know the extent and nature of his love? How can we know his will for us? Kant's natural law was a rejection of the entire Biblical narrative, a denial of story after story of God's involvement with his world.

Just as problematic is the very concept of a natural law. Did man really observe some kind of universal morality? Did human history reveal such a thing? Was kindness, humility and self-giving our 'natural' state? The Enlightenment, unbound from history, couldn't be bothered with such questions. It was too busy blazing a path towards a great new future to ever look back or for that matter to take a good look at itself. Yet another question Kant ignored with his organizing principle, how could he be sure this God, discovered by means of this natural law, wasn't simply a projection of his own mind?

Only a few people may refer to themselves today as Kantian in their beliefs, but philosophy has a way of shedding its philosophical underpinnings and working its way into mainstream thought. Passed down from Kant's and Descartes' pure subjectivity, we now hear such statements as "this is my truth," an utterance the authors of the Old and New Testaments as well as classical Greek philosophers would have considered incoherent. The secular world dismisses out of hand the notion that God can reveal himself. Modern religious impulses, thoroughly indoctrinated by the Enlightenment, believe God can somehow be found in our self-reflections or inner spirituality. Even without its formal title, natural law has become part of today's furniture despite its deep contradictions. Natural law silently stands behind the claims of our social scientists and our politicians, telling us we can build an ethical and peaceful world, one always just around the corner. If we enact enough programs we can achieve their great vision, ignoring the fact that the man they speak of is both hypothetical and ahistorical. Their solutions are dependent upon the metrics of our disciplines of science, yet they always remain at a distance from the innate spirit and needs of man. Caught up in his own enthusiasm, Kant wrote that this bright new world of peace and harmony would soon come to pass, perhaps he mused, in his own lifetime.

Georg Wilhelm Friedrich Hegel (1770-1831) became, along with Kant, the second giant of the Enlightenment. So well-known in academic circles, he's referred to simply as Hegel, with like-minded people called Hegelians. Like his predecessors, Hegel's philosophy was a reflection of the age. During his lifetime Europe was reaching even greater heights, surpassing all other cultures in industry, learning and science. Hegel asked a question of this ascendance, "why us and why is this happening now?"

His was the question of human progress, as Hegel firmly believed his time and his culture was on the cusp of history's grand culmination. In looking for answers concerning his questions of progress, he looked back to antiquity, civilizations such as ancient Mesopotamia, classical Greece and Rome. He wondered what propelled them forward, yet at other times he asked what held them back? Reflecting the boundless optimism of the Enlightenment era, Hegel attempted to construct nothing less than a philosophy which would explain all of human history. Taking for example ancient Greece, he saw a progressive leap forward in its polis or city state, which granted each male citizen full democratic rights. But Hegel saw progress as proceeding in fits and starts, yet with an inevitable trajectory towards man's absolute freedom and self-awareness. So why did the first Greek democracy collapse? He attributed each civilization's failure to what he termed 'contradictions.' Greek citizens possessed the right to fully participate in government, but Greece also accepted slavery. That was its contradiction, holding it back and eventually leading to its collapse.

Hegel's most radical claim wasn't his philosophy of history. It was his claim that there was a force behind this human process, what he called Geist, loosely translated from his German language as meaning 'spirit.' Whether this spirit was the hand of God or some collective human consciousness moving the world forward, he left vague. Likely it was a mixture of both. Hegel identified three elements at work through this Geist-spirit: thesis, anthesis and synthesis. The status quo of a culture was its thesis, but as its contradictions grew, an anthesis arose in the form of internal unrest or conflict with other civilizations, leading to the toppling of the thesis. Emerging from this process were new ideas and higher truths, now reformulated. This became his synthesis, the means by which man was evolving towards his appointed end. Hegel termed all of this his dialectical process.

Hegel's ideas were an immediate sensation, especially in academic circles. His enthusiastic acceptance may be explained in part by a philosophy of flattery which reflected Europe's growing sense of cultural superiority. Now he asked, why was Europe the one culture approaching this pinnacle of history? Hegel supplied the last piece of the puzzle in the form of Christianity. The Christian God, he claimed, was leading Western civilization out of its contradictions into its final synthesis. Hegel's God was anything but orthodox however. In his philosophy, man was not the only one evolving in this dialectical progression, so was God. Strangely God himself was caught up in this process, moving towards his own ultimate state of freedom and self-awareness. The Enlightenment dagger was now firmly placed into the Christian Church. A God who required his own evolution was a lesser god brought down to earth, one who walked alongside man. He was no longer transcendent.

Like other philosophical projects, they eventually shed themselves of their philosophers and make their way into modern thought. Today our secular world advances this notion of a constant evolution of mankind, leading to some great end, while ignoring history's ups and downs. Hegel's voice can be heard by leaders evoking the arc of history, placing all our hopes in our scientific and technological advances. Man again perfecting man. Hegel left us with other legacies. With his dialectical process of thesis, anthesis and synthesis, all beliefs and truth-claims are subject to never-ending negotiation and renegotiation. In process history there is no overarching objective truth upon which we can rely, nothing is fixed and stable. Everything is culturally conditioned, simply a reflection of current thinking.

Hegel left us something else, Karl Marx (1818-1883). Descartes had moved God into the subjective realm. Kant had placed morality solely in the sphere of human ways, while Hegel relegated God to someone less than perfect. Now that the Enlightenment had edged God to the edge of the cliff, Marx was able to push him off with ease, a move which only decades earlier seemed impossible for a culture. Marx was enthralled with Hegel's philosophy of progress, but as an avowed atheist and materialist, he tossed aside the Geist-spirit. For

Marx the opposing force of anthesis, holding mankind back from greatness, was to be found in economics. Our essence he claimed, existed in our creativity, whether an artist's painting or a factory worker's finished product. Capitalism he believed swooped in and appropriated our creative essence with its pursuit of profit. In yet another series of grand Enlightenment utopian promises, Marx believed the elimination of capital and profit would become our final synthesis. This was the Communist revolution's workers' paradise.

Should anyone doubt the power of philosophy with its quasi-religious claims, Marx's ideas once held captive half the world. Communist art gave Marxist thought its artistic and quasi-religious expression with its murals and posters portraying the universal worker, men and women with sleeves rolled up, gazing with bold expressions upward into the horizon, envisioning this great new future. Such was the Geist-spirit sold to the masses, unable to see what was really beyond the Godless horizon, the mass starvations, the gulags and the secret police.

In looking back the Enlightenment was an easy sell. It gave us a new man standing on the summit, the serpent's promise to be like god. Perhaps that was the deepest irony of the Enlightenment promise in its attempt to show us new heights. It could never approach the heights of the Judeo-Christian vision of mankind. We were made in the image of God.

What of Friedrich Nietzsche (1844-1900), still influential today and still revered in academic circles? We're familiar with his animosity towards religion, but Nietzsche denounced the Enlightenment as well. He saw both the man of religion and the man of reason as feeble and weak, attaching themselves only to myth. According to Nietzsche, man could only infuse his life with meaning through pure action. Only by boldly seizing power and reshaping the world to his own ends, could man actualize himself. Faith, with its appeal to humility and love, was seen as impotent; incapable of allowing man to achieve his true nature, but so was the Enlightenment appeal to reason.

Even if we reject Nietzsche's atheism, he proved to be an insightful critic of his time. In his book 'The Gay Science,' Nietzsche's madman character roams the streets shouting, "God is dead." This was more than Nietzsche's signature statement concerning faith. It was also his reflection upon a European culture that had distanced itself from Christianity in its embrace of the Enlightenment. Seduced by Kant and Hegel, he saw a Europe shed of one myth only to reach out for another. Nietzsche's madman saw the West, having cast off its faith, as more lost than ever. Henceforth he saw European man having to look into the dark abyss of death with only reason by his side. For Nietzsche, the madman's cry was a form of lament, for a Europe that had abandoned its only historical form of hope. In the next chapter we will see what happened when Europe looked down into that abyss.

Chapter Four

Out of the Rubble

Jeremiah 17:9 The heart is devious above all else; it is perverse – who can understand it?

The Enlightenment declared man free, free of God and free of tradition, governed only by his own self. As is often the case with grand philosophical projects, assumptions went unexamined and reality soon impinged. As Jeremiah reminds us, this emancipated man did not take into account his dark side.

In the aftermath of two World Wars, Western man sat in the rubble of Berlin. He was starving in a Siberian gulag. He witnessed the charred bodies of Auschwitz. With millions dead on the battlefield, the survivors were confronted with questions. Where was this man of reason? Was this our natural law? What happened to the grand new future Hegel promised? War couldn't be blamed on a few zealots, although in time that's the lie we would tell ourselves. Millions raised their arms to their Fuhrer. Millions remained silent as the Jewish people were herded into boxcars. Neighbor turned in neighbor to the Soviet secret police. It wasn't psychopaths who ran the concentration camps. For the most part they were bankers, clerks and merchants, people like us who were simply entranced by the promised glory of a new time and a new man.

The Church found itself compromised as well. Long before the World Wars, it had abandoned much of its foundations, trying to get with the times and embrace the spirit of the age. Ceasing to be countercultural, it no longer enjoined men and women to pick up their cross. Instead it became something watered down, undemanding and often nationalistic. The new Church was unable to summon Europe away from the abyss and into repentance.

Sitting in the rubble, Europe faced a choice. What was the way forward? All cultures require some shared ideals, necessary to keep the ever present threat of chaos at arm's length. Those ideals and principles may be true or false, weak or strong. For Europe two roads lay ahead. One was the way home, reclaiming its Christian roots, the faith which had pulled it out of the Dark Ages into a great civilization, not just scientifically, economically and artistically, but at its best with a unique sensibility towards the worth of the individual. With its constant call to repentance, Christianity was the honest self-assessment it needed, but it would require a return to an authentic and demanding faith, not the self-serving one it had fashioned for itself. It was still possible to come home.

The other road was much like the one it had just traveled, repeating the enticing lies of the Enlightenment, just repackaged in a more nuanced way. By taking this road, Europe would avoid looking into the mirror, giving man permission to look up the sky amid the carnage and declare God guilty. Discretely it would absolve Nazism and Communism of their abject atheism. Sitting in the rubble they could cry out, "Where was God?," while failing to ask "Where were we?"

Still burdened by its Enlightenment mindset, Europe was unable to take a sober look at itself, adopting yet another human centric philosophy. It was given the name postmodernism, and over time it became even more deceptive than its predecessor. Like all grand lies, it would wrap itself in half-truths and elevated rhetoric. Looking around and seeing the devastation of war and a once great culture run amok, postmodernism would declare itself hostile to the very idea of strong culture. Rather than traveling down the road of reforming the West, reclaiming its cultural strengths, it would now set fire to them.

Postmodernism initially presented itself under the seemingly benign guise of radical pluralism, although in time it would impose its own suffocating ideology. American philosopher Richard Rorty (1931-2007) articulated the essence of postmodern thought, "The higher truth for any man is what he believes it to be." No longer were there any objective or eternal truths, whether Christian or Enlightenment, as both were discarded. Any convictions of right or wrong, good or bad, beautiful or base depended upon the perspective of the individual, or for some postmodernists, the perspective of a community.

My truth is mine and yours is yours, a statement any classical Greek philosopher or Biblical writer would have found incomprehensible. By another name postmodern philosophy would also be called relativism or moral relativism. This new truth, if you can call it that, was by its nature ever-changing, depending upon time, place and current thinking. On its face postmodernism declared all prior philosophical or religious projects dead. No one could say anything universal, except however for the postmodernists who declared themselves as the judge of all others. By its own terms it was incapable of providing the answers historically provided by culture, who am I, what is the good life or how should we live together? Such human questions were no longer asked, confined in vague terms to each person's conscience. Stripped of its rhetoric, it eventually revealed itself to be only a means of tearing down, a power grab by elite intellectuals and marginal politicians who were, until now, on the outside looking in. Here in the rubble they saw their opportunity.

Enthralled with its ascent, postmodernism didn't realize it wasn't all that new. In reality it was a rehash of a long-discarded Greek philosophy prior to Socrates, advanced by a group called Sophists of the Fifth and Sixth Century B.C. They also claimed truth was only what a person or group claimed it to be with its most famous proponent Protagoras declaring, "Man is the measure of all things." Much of classical Greek philosophy, once a foundation of Western thought, was an extended argument in fierce opposition to the Sophists with Socrates, Plato and Aristotle all seeing relative truth for what it was, a cancer not only upon culture but upon mankind's soul as well.

Postmodernism had an initial appeal beyond its narcissistic lure. By declaring strong culture as a threat, whether Aryan or Soviet, it sought to silence any future threats that could lead to a form of totalitarianism. With its advocacy of weak culture, or no culture, relativism appeared to silence the drumbeat of war, colonialism and the other excesses of the past. But such criticism was misdirected. It wasn't the drumbeat of Western culture which led it into war. It was the West's departure from its Christian past, the godlessness of Nazism and Communism. Also lost on postmodernism was the fact that it required the strong culture of the Allies to win both World Wars. Now with culture weakened, the West is steadily losing its will to summon any action in the face of external threats or internal challenges.

It also had another opponent to eliminate and that was faith. In Christianity's assertion of a universal and ultimate truth, relativism recognized its supreme rival. Unable to counter the ability of faith to supply us with our answers for living, postmodernism reached for its blunt instrument, a constant nihilistic assault upon the Church.

Although postmodernism claimed to dismiss the philosophy of the Enlightenment, it turned out to be a close relative. Both rejected tradition. Both appealed to the subjective individual for their respective truths. Each in their own way embraced Kant's natural law, with man as a source of his own ethics. The cumulative cost of both ideologies upon the West, especially Europe, is becoming evident, now mired in a deep malaise, not just economically and socially, but spiritually. Weak culture and postmodernism was the spirit in which the European Union was conceived and created, seeking to blur national identities, while at the same time it soundly rejected any reference in its charter to Europe's religious history. Without the cultural answers faith provides, the West also lost its dynamism in literature, art and other cultural expressions. In a world where only the self is exalted, there is nothing truly great to declare.

One of the postmodern ways of tearing down is called 'deconstruction.' Using this method, the postmodernist tears apart, sentence by sentence, all historical writings, claiming to unmask their underlying agendas of power and oppression, whether Christian, white, colonial or capitalist. Dethroning oppressive social structures is a worthy endeavor, but postmodern deconstruction reveals nothing other than its own grab for dominance. It destroys yet posits nothing it its place. It scorches the earth of anything other than itself, without any discernment as to which cultural traits we should preserve. As the severe judge of all else, it unmasked itself as just another power move.

As the grand arbiter, postmodernism is incapable of self-examination, unable to ask itself even the most basic questions. By declaring that there's no such thing as objective truth, isn't such a statement in itself a declaration of something as absolutely true? If truth is determined by the individual or by a local community, logically it follows that the postmodern truth is no higher or more valid than a racist truth, an Aryan truth or a whole host of other evils.

Over time relativism evolved into the kind of ideology it once pretended to condemn. With its deconstruction of tradition, it eventually established its own monolithic culture. The first wave came from the intellectual elites of the university, passed down to students as the first acolytes carrying the message into the upheavals of the 1960s, railing against the 'system' and any other form of authority. Initially moral relativism said no one could question another's truth claim, allowing the true believers to congratulate themselves on their openness, toleration and inclusivity, but such a stance could not hold. Ideas always compete for both prominence and power. Once postmodernism gained its foothold, especially on college campuses, its noncritical stance gave way to zealous crusades, the control of thought and language in its attempt to eliminate any rivals. Now one has to choose their words carefully to avoid their methods of shaming, censorship, boycotts and threats of job loss. Offenders are subject to sensitivity training, but only their sensitivities. Opposition isn't met with dialogue but with reeducation, since no other point of view can possibly be right. The result of this new culture is a social and political arena in which ideas can no longer compete or compromise, leaving us with only rigid ideological stances unable to provide solutions to our complex problems.

Postmodernism has taken the Enlightenment man to his ultimate expression. Man alone, autonomous, standing in a universe we didn't create, unaware of our origin and unable to control our destiny, announces himself as its master. He is the prideful man leaping into the Grand Canyon, declaring himself free from gravity. This self-transcendent man without a past is also one without a future, caught up only in the distractions of now with our constant technological noise. Incapable of reflection and with no future, perhaps this noise is his only refuge.

Despite modernity's takeover, humans will always be human. Our longings and yearnings may be suppressed yet they can never be lost. Because we sense in our deepest selves a spirit, we will eventually turn back. We are, by our nature, seekers of meaning and purpose, of matters far beyond those things we can bestow upon ourselves. Our parade of ideologies and our technology will never fill the void. Our deepest intuitions will always turn us back towards the truth about us and the great heights we intuit. We are made in the image of God. Mystery still surrounds, not only when we look up at the night sky, but whenever we look within.

Chapter Five

Secular Humanists: Who Are They?

Luke 10:21 At that same hour Jesus rejoiced in the Holy Spirit and said, "I thank you, Father, Lord of heaven and earth, because you have hidden these things from the wise and the intelligent and have revealed them to infants; yes, Father, for such was your gracious will.

In any conversation, whether religious or political, it's unlikely you'll find someone who refers to themselves as a secular humanist. Most people don't know what the term means. Yet for millions if not a majority of the West, it has become something of a religion by default. Those who do call themselves secular humanists prefer to be called by the title 'humanists,' likely unaware that this term has long since been taken by a Fourteen and Fifteenth Century European movement which gave the Renaissance its beginnings. Hoping to breathe new life into a pessimistic view of man which arose out of the Middle Ages, these humanists set out to elevate the individual to the heights originally envisioned by Christianity by fusing faith with the classical works of Greece and Rome. That's another of the endless ironies of secular humanism. As it attempts to distance itself from the past, it freely borrows from it. Still another irony, secular humanism's view of man has returned us to an ancient vision both cold and lifeless.

What Do They Believe?

The core beliefs of secular humanism can be found in the following statement adopted by the International Humanist and Ethical Union: "Humanism is a democratic and ethical life stance, which affirms that human beings have the right and responsibility to give meaning and shape to their own lives. It stands for the building of a more humane society through an ethic based on human and other natural values in the spirit of reason and free inquiry though human capabilities. It is not theistic and it does not accept supernatural views of reality."

Using such terms as democratic, ethical and humane, this sounds like an attractive way of life. Who can disagree with building a better world? But now that we've lived in their secular experiment for several decades, their claim of a better world is crumbling at the edges. Still, their words are noble and their abstractions admirable, until you near the end of their belief statement, "It is not theistic." That of course means they exclude any belief in God, a vast point of departure for the Judeo-Christian believer, which begs a question upon which all rises or falls. Can we, on our own and apart from God, build this ethical and humane world they speak of?

History presents us with a long list of the sins of the Church, but history also presents us with something far more insidious. The secular humanist project, the promised good without God, has already been tried many times over. This was the call of the French Revolution with the sacking of Churches, the murder of priests, its prisons and guillotine. This was the promise of the Soviet Union's vast totalitarian state of fear and control. This was the Chinese Cultural Revolution which left tens of millions dead. The secular call to good without God, gave us a Twentieth Century carnage surpassing all other centuries combined. Now clothed in muted tones, it returns with the same promise. As Fyodor Dostoyevsky wrote, "When God is absent, all is permitted."

In addition to their belief statement, the United States Secular Humanist Society has published the following four principles:

"Dogma, ideology and traditions whether religious, political or social must be weighed and tested by each individual and not simply accepted by faith." Here you can see the legacy of the Enlightenment with its postmodern twist; the individual determining what is true on his or her own terms. Its deep contradictions are apparent. In rejecting any universal ideology and defaulting to our personal viewpoint, secular humanism attempts to advance its own universal and dogmatic form of truth. Also, with its deep suspicion of tradition, secular humanism has penned its own suicide note. The individual of the future, who will weigh everything by their own preferences, can easily toss aside these principles.

"We are committed to the use of critical reason and scientific method of inquiry, in seeking solutions to human problems." Again this is a recycling of the Enlightenment in its ultimate appeal to reason and science. By enlisting science, it's a clever attempt to leverage a philosophical stance to unassailable heights, but the secular experiment and its repeated failures, has already shown us that the most basic of human problems ultimately cannot be solved by reason or by science.

"A conviction that with reason and an open exchange of ideas and tolerance, progress can be made in building a better world." Here is a return of the utopian promises we've encountered before. Much like the Enlightenment, we have to assume a hypothetical man of pure reason, devoid of ego and self-interest, a man who has yet to exist. How can this self, who by nature seeks itself, lead us to this better world?

"With the present state of scientific knowledge, dogmatic belief in an absolute moral system is unreasonable. However it affirms that individuals engaging in rational deliberation can discuss some universal objective standards." Natural law makes its return, the same natural law which gave us two World Wars. Having come full circle, we ask, how can science give us a moral system? How can particle colliders and test tubes show us what is ethical and right? Also unanswered is how these individuals, bound by nothing other than their own subjective belief systems, can arrive at anything universal?

Justice Anthony Kennedy, writing for the majority in the 1992 Supreme Court decision of Planned Parenthood v. Casey, may have provided the most eloquent expression of secular humanism: "At the heart of liberty is the right to define one's own existence, of meaning, of the universe and of the mystery of life." He is the jurist born of the Enlightenment. According to his mantra, laws are not cohesive ways of binding us, nor does religion, culture or any of our institutions inform and shape us. Instead, this new self-defining man, cut off from tradition and its accumulated wisdom, cut off from any outside influence whether family, faith or the past, determines who he is. This new self-constituted modern man, blazing his own glorious path inward, is directionless.

Who Are They?

Years ago I was a part of a group that called itself Interfaith. We met downtown every month for the purpose of discussing religious questions in the context of different faiths. Discussions however ended up having little to do with religion; instead it became a rehash of current cultural trends. For the majority, there was no such thing as Biblical authority, its status was no greater than any other work of literature. It was too old and remote to be of relevance in our modern world. The resurrection was rejected out of hand; there was no science or reason behind it. Much of our time was spent recounting the failings of the Church without any recognition of the millions it fed and consoled every day. Christian doctrine was a form of indoctrination, not something for free thinkers. After a few sessions, I privately renamed it Interdoubt.

What struck me so deeply wasn't the secular thought process of the group reflecting the times, but the fact that most of them were of my age group, in their sixties, raised by Depression era parents who were thoroughly churched. Listening to our discussions, I kept thinking to myself, how did this revolution happen so quickly, how did it become so deeply entrenched? Only one other member represented what I considered an orthodox Christian point of view. Initially we saw ourselves as the foil and counterweight, but over time the secular humanist voice became so prevalent, I sat back, taking mental notes of this spirit of the age.

A few stories will give you a sense. During one meeting I remarked that the Gospels had a way of demanding a decision from the reader, citing Jesus' parables which placed us in a crossroad and crisis. If you didn't accept a wedding invitation, there were consequences. Seeds sown either grew on fertile soil or they withered and died. If you didn't bring enough oil for your lamp, you were shut out. Even a failure to decide turned out to be a decision in itself. My comments raised an exchange of glances and raised eyebrows. I could tell from the ensuing discussion that such absolute demands by any external authority, was a modern day heresy, an infringement upon our sacred sense of freedom. One of the members even remarked it was dangerous.

Knowing most of them were members of a Church, I decided upon a rejoinder in the form of a question, "When you recite the first Commandment, to love God with all your heart, all your mind and all your soul, what does that mean to you?" A few vague comments followed, but nothing approaching an answer. I saw in their relative silence something of the secular stance. It would not accept any absolutes of God, yet at the same time it lacked the courage to reject him. Theirs was the illusion of some middle ground, a safe place to stand by constructing their own god with their own set of ethics, a construction which faced another Biblical challenge from the words of Christ, "Believe in me."

At another meeting the moderator presented to the group a New York Times bestselling book. The author's premise was to ask what Jesus would have done, had he not been crucified. According to the writer, this older Jesus would have followed much the same path as Mohammad, turning to more radical methods. I wasn't quite sure how to proceed in a discussion of this non-existent alternate universe, but rather than hold up the absurdity of the premise, I decided to hold up a tacit discrimination of secular humanism. I asked, "Are you also saying that if Gandhi or Martin Luther King had lived longer, they too would have been tossing Molotov cocktails in the streets?" That was of course off limits for discussion, as it should be. But it met its mark, exposing the modern prejudice of Jesus as fair game for any and all of our cultural agendas or projections.

One other session revealed a core idea of secular humanist thought. Serving as the moderator that month, I presented a book by Soren Kierkegaard in which he considered the story of Abraham's sacrifice of Isaac from the Book of Genesis. Abraham and Sarah, too old to have a child, clung desperately for years to God's promise of a son, finally receiving their blessing in the form of Isaac. Kierkegaard found God's later demand for the sacrifice of Isaac to be a story of unfathomable depths. As I set the stage for discussion, recounting the scene of Abraham holding his knife above Isaac, I posed to them a series of questions. The group wouldn't dip a toe into the story's deep waters. My questions were met with complete silence.

Sill hoping to foster some discussion, I pointed out that Genesis made it clear from the outset that God's demand was only a test. He didn't want Isaac's life. He wanted to know what was in Abraham's heart. Abraham was the one person on Earth chosen by God to carry out his covenant promise for the world's salvation. Given this supreme and demanding task, would he be obedient to God's word, or would Abraham in his own personal Enlightenment, refuse God by substituting his own conscience and his own ethics? God needed to know. Eventually one person in our group spoke up, and as far as I could tell he was speaking for the rest, "This isn't my God." In a sense he was right. This wasn't the human-centric god upon whom we could cast our own sense of right and wrong, a god we could easily fit into our culture. This small god would demand nothing of us.

This is the stealth which underlies secular humanism. It will call itself religious, it will even go to Church, but silently it holds up orthodox religion to a higher governing belief system of its own.

Belief is in name only, sorted, sifted and recast through the prism of reason, science and man.

What Are Their Ways of Persuasion?

Now that we've looked at some secular humanist beliefs, we now turn to their often beguiling ways of persuasion. I learned something about their methods up close from my alma mater, Vanderbilt University. When I was there in the early 1970s, the university projected the image of a liberal bastion rising above its southern roots, but most of us considered this a reflection of Ivy League envy more than anything else. Other than a few anti-war protesters, during my years it was a traditional school with traditional students.

Forty years later, serving on the board of a local campus ministry, I found it to be a very different place. The campus minister opened one of our meetings with an ominous tone, relaying her conversation with the administration from the week before, a conversation which didn't bode well for our organization. She told us about a recent controversy involving a Christian fraternity, Beta Upsilon Chi, known as the Bucs. One of its members was an openly gay student, but evidently this didn't present a problem, since the fraternity's oath regarding sexual conduct consisted only of a pledge of celibacy outside of marriage.

The controversy arose when the student declared that he would no longer be bound by his pledge, eventually leading to his dismissal from the fraternity. I hoped this step was reached only after a long and thoughtful attempt at reconciliation, but I learned that straight students had previously been ousted under the same standard. When the university learned of his dismissal, its relentless machinery began to grind its opponents, real or perceived, under its gears. Bucs was immediately kicked off campus, without appeal. But the real agenda was revealed a few weeks later, as a series of edicts were handed down by the administration. Henceforth, every registered student organization, known as RSOs, was required to submit its charter and bylaws to the university, and two primary rules would determine whether they could remain on campus.

The first was called the 'all comers rule.' According to the administration, membership in each RSO must be open to everyone, regardless of its makeup or purpose. Absurd results come to mind, such as a pacifist joining the ROTC, but that didn't matter. Seizing the controversy as an opportunity to impose its sweeping social agenda was all that mattered. The second rule was dubbed the 'leadership rule.' All RSO elections must be open to anyone, without any qualification concerning beliefs. These high-minded principles, however, would not apply to the administration, faculty or staff. For one, the University Club was not open to all comers.

The initial reaction of Christian students was one of bewilderment. Their organizations had done nothing wrong. For decades they had quietly carried out their missions without controversy. As questions began to mount from the RSOs, wanting either explanations or clarifications, the university announced that it would address all these issues in a town hall gathering. The university was represented at the meeting by a three person panel, a provost, its chief legal counsel and the dean of the divinity school. Lasting almost two hours, I found the relative silence of the divinity school dean somewhat revealing. Still, he may have served his purpose by sitting at the table. It tacitly said to the students that enlightened religion was on the university's side.

The provost opened by delivering his remarks to a standing room audience of mostly Christian students. He began with the predictable fare, invoking mutual understanding and an open exchange of ideas. But the machine soon revealed itself with his following remarks, "But I want to make it clear that the new rules for RSOs will not be changed or repealed." This was their open exchange, the enlightened view handed down to the unenlightened. Like so many secular projects, behind their nice sounding rhetoric it says 'submit.'

The chief legal officer added his own comments, saying the law required the university to implement the new rules. Several weeks later, following the submission of several legal briefs on behalf of the RSOs, his claim turned out to be patently false. There was no such legal requirement, all of which raises a question. Even if they mistakenly thought it was necessary, why would such a noble crusade hide behind the law as a pretext?

During the ensuing question and answer session, I was impressed by the passion of the students as well as their ability to articulate their faith. Following several initial questions critical of the university's overreaching, the provost suddenly declared to the assembled crowd that they weren't representative of the general campus sentiment. How he was able to discern this from those who were absent was unclear, but his invocation of a non-existent majority was a postmodernist position. The truth of the matter wasn't the truth of the matter; instead it somehow relied upon a consensus of some sort. Principles were not principles unless there was this vague form of agreement among the enlightened.

One student, a football player who was also an officer in the Fellowship of Christian Athletes, stood up to address the panel, "The FCA is fine with the all-comers policy. We're open to anyone who wants to join. But as far as the leadership rule, how can we carry out our mission of leading people to Christ, if the leader doesn't even believe in Christ?" He laid bare the absurdities of their ideological rule-making world, but secular humanism, perceiving itself situated on an enlightened and elevated plain, doesn't believe it has to answer. The chief legal officer cleverly sidestepped, reaching instinctively as secularism often does, for a catchphrase. "Aren't you open to new ideas?" The power of sloganeering, with its ability to end a discussion rather than engender further thought, caught the student momentarily off guard. Who could respond by saying they aren't open to new ideas?

With just a moment's reflection, the answer is obvious. Of course Christians are open to new ideas. The Church, as the most diverse of all institutions, has historically embraced new ideas and new cultures around the world. It established the first universities; it was the first to institutionalize hundreds of social justice movements from anti-slavery movements to workers' rights. But the real answer is this:

don't we first examine new ideas before we adopt them? Don't we ask of new ideas, is this true or false, is this right or wrong? Are we so enamored with the word 'new' we now fail to ask such questions? Would the University accept a new idea threatening its own mission as it asks of these RSOs?

Realizing the discussion wasn't headed towards any type of consensus, the provost tried to be bridge the gap by sharing his own religious thoughts, "Look I go to Church, but I don't take my beliefs with me to the university." His apparent attempt to find some common ground was met with an audible gasp, as the provost looked around the auditorium, evidently surprised by the students' reaction. The ensuing silence said all that needed to be said. No bridge could be built between these two worlds. His statement reflected not only a profound misunderstanding of Christianity, but of all religious traditions. How can someone claim to believe in a God who is Creator, Sustainer and Destiny of all things, only to lay this God aside, isolated to a corner of one's life? Who is this god of the secular world? At one time did he go by the name of Zeus or Apollo? His was of course a mishmash of Enlightenment and postmodern views, the supreme individual who determines for themselves their own god and its boundaries.

A female student rose from her seat to reply, saying in an economy of words something so true, "But my faith is who I am." She couldn't conceive of this small modern god, any more than the provost could conceive of her infinite God. She couldn't understand a life so self-directed, so bifurcated and so lacking in unity. Taking her seat, apparently not expecting a response, the provost wore a blank expression, finally blurting out in a halting manner, "Well I'm happy for you." Likely it was only a sense of propriety which prevented someone in the crowd from shouting out, "Is that all you got?"

Even if you did call this a dialogue, both sides spoke different languages. With an uncomfortable silence gathering over the auditorium, one of the panelists tried to restart the process, "Well, let's talk about the implementation of the new rules." A few minutes later a student raised his hand to ask, "Will the rules be published so we can understand how we're supposed to comply?" The same panelist shot back no, they would be administered on an ad hoc basis, claiming "too many permutations" for rules to be written. This is an odd response from an institution which promulgates a wide and endless range of rules and regulations, from sexual conduct to academic integrity. In short the rules would be whatever they said.

Finally one student stood to express his general frustration of having these guidelines shoved down their throats, with the chief legal counsel responding, "We're only asking you to comply with the new policy. It doesn't govern your private conscience." Presumably in the name of tolerance, the Christian students would be allowed to believe what they wanted to believe, as long as it was confined to their thoughts. Lost to the panel was the obvious hypocrisy. The university wasn't confined to its thoughts. Its ideology must be enforced. This demonstrated still another profound misunderstanding, perhaps even antagonism, towards religion. Authentic faith in all traditions isn't confined to our inner thoughts. It's meant to be lived out and shared. Our light is supposed to shine rather than hidden under a basket. What sort of faith, believing its truths are a source of meaning and joy, would be so devoid of love for our neighbor that it would withhold itself in silence? Maybe there is an intuitive agenda at work here. In carrying out the Post-Christian project of silencing all rivals, perhaps it knows any faith so confined will recede into obscurity. Maybe this imposed silence could be the means by which they hope it will wither and die.

Epilogue

Fourteen campus organizations were eventually kicked off campus. One group, the Christian Legal Society, submitted its charter for approval, containing the following statement, "Each officer of the Christian Legal Society is expected to lead Bible study, prayer and worship at meetings." With its rejection notice, the following reply came from the university, "This seems to indicate that officers are expected to hold some sort of belief. Vanderbilt University policy does not allow this as a qualifier." From its self-perceived heights, it couldn't see the absurdity of such a statement. Everyone operates under 'some sort of belief,' including the beliefs of the administration and in this case beliefs that must be followed.

Academic circles like to read from the old postmodern script, claiming each person's own personal truth is equally valid, but the sweeping decrees of the university tells us that modernity has abandoned any such pretense. Human beings are by nature worshipping beings, consciously or unconsciously seeking to attach our finite selves to something higher. That 'something higher' may not be all that transcendent, sometimes taking the form of political causes or ideologies, sometimes it's only a reflection of our egos. For this reason, postmodernism in its initial form could never hold, having now mutated into its own rigorous belief system, complete with its own idols.

There's one more story to tell. The RSO controversy was short-lived. Local newspapers gave it scant attention, relegating it to the back pages. In a city once calling itself a part of the Bible belt, there was little protest. Only a few alumni registered their complaints, as things soon settled down into a silence which spoke more clearly than any town hall meeting. Loud and clear it proclaimed that the revolution had seized the high ground.

Chapter Six

The Altar of Science

Psalm 8:3 When I look at your heavens, the work of your fingers, the moon and the stars that you have established; what are human beings that you are mindful of them, mortals that you care for them? Yet you have made them a little lower than God, and crowned them with glory and honor.

Can faith and science coexist? It's a question often asked today, but for the greater part of Western Civilization's long history, it wasn't a problem. In fact, for centuries the Church and science reinforced one another. Persons of faith such as Isaac Newton, Albert Einstein, Blaise Pascal, Galileo and many others saw no contradictions.

As a Christian, I accept anything science demonstrates by way of the scientific method. Faith shouldn't be about denying facts; instead it should be about looking beyond the facts into deeper truths which science, within its own boundaries, cannot approach. The debate today stems not from any real conflict between the Church and science, but something new that I call pseudoscience. With its secular agenda, pseudoscience attempts to hijack real science, making philosophical or quasi-religious claims. This may be the most powerful tool of agnostics, potent because it attempts to leverage itself with the certainty of science while making unscientific claims. The Christian response should be thoughtful and it should also be rational. We may assert truths beyond the realm of science, but that doesn't mean we should be denying the benefits of science. In order to cut through some modern day confusion, we need to understand this new phenomenon of pseudoscience and what it claims.

Who Kept the Flame?

Before we engage with pseudoscience, we need to correct a historical narrative which casts the Church as a traditional enemy of science. The Catholic Church did in fact reject the Copernican revolution, and it placed Galileo under house arrest. There was a point in time when the Church tied its theology too closely to science, but this is a very thin slice of history, a snapshot without context or balance. The far larger historical narrative tells us that it was the Church who kept the flame of scientific knowledge alive for Western civilization, providing it with the spark leading to its eventual ascendance.

After the fall of Rome, Europe plunged into the Dark Ages. For those living in such times, the idea of progress was a foreign concept as they looked back to ancient Greece and Rome as the pinnacle of civilization now lost. During this period both the Far East and the Middle East surpassed Europe in all areas of invention and scholarship. But the West later underwent an explosion of science and innovation, one which still reverberates to this day. The vast majority of advances in physics, medicine, space travel and thousands of other discoveries we know today, all originated from the West. Were the people of the West smarter? Of course not, revealing to us something about the power and influence of culture.

What sparked this unprecedented scientific revolution of the West? Many factors were at work, but with the collapse of the Roman Empire, followed by a fractured European culture consisting of rival feudal states, one has to ask: who kept the flame of knowledge alive? If knowledge cannot leap forward from zero, what enabled this explosion? The answer is the monastery system, with thousands of abbeys and cloisters dotting the European continent. They were the only institutions of the time engaged in the disciplines of math, science and philosophy. Monks and abbots made up the majority of the literate class, housing in their libraries the accumulated knowledge of Egypt, Greece and Rome. All the great universities of Europe, Oxford, Cambridge, the University of Paris and others, emerged from the Church and the monastic tradition.

There is another less tangible reason for the scientific ascendance of the West, a European mind infused with the mind of Christianity. As the West leapt forward in science, both the Middle East and Far East began to recede. Each of them began to further isolate themselves from the outside world. The difference in the Western worldview towards science can best be demonstrated by a comparison to other worldviews, in this case we will examine the Hindu viewpoint.

For the Hindu, humankind is caught up in the recurring Samsara wheel of life. Death threw one back into the wheel, casting us out again either as a different person or in a different form. Only a few spiritual elites could escape. The difference in scientific view was engendered by a difference in the perception of ultimate reality. To the Hindu our knowledge of an absolute and infinite god, beyond their local gods, was completely inaccessible. You couldn't peer behind the curtain. The cosmos was impenetrable. This barrier made for an uneasy marriage of faith and science. If reality was in the final analysis unapproachable and therefore mystical, could science say anything definitive? In a similar manner Islam began to distance itself from science as a group of Imams long ago discouraged science, claiming that the Koran supplied mankind with all necessary knowledge. In prior African and Native American cultures, nature was infused with spirits. With the sky, the water and the mountains spiritualized, there was no means by which one could consider laws by which they would be governed.

Christianity engendered a different mindset with a belief in a personal God. This meant the West projected upon God something akin to a mind, as well as someone who revealed himself. This also meant the universe, as a product of this mind, was rational. It would have order and it would obey fixed laws. With God accessible and his order placed before us, Western science assumed it could understand the physical world. Reality was not impenetrable. We could lift the veil at least partially. In this manner the West saw itself assembling pieces of a puzzle, as Christian faith and science proved to be a good marriage. Einstein, who was able to see this imposed order of God imprinted upon the universe, gave this concept perhaps its best expression, "The most incomprehensible thing about the universe, is that it is comprehensible."

Prove It

With history now purged of some modern propaganda, let's return to the larger question concerning faith and science. Two words, spoken on two different occasions, caused me think about this question. The two words were 'prove it.' The first occasion was a lecture at a local university, delivered by a professor of religion. While explaining Karl Bart's theology of revelation, a young divinity school student threw up her hand and with an air of protest in her voice, "How can you prove any of that?" I'll return to her question, as well as the professor's response, later in this chapter.

The other time was at an Interfaith meeting. As we were discussing the different Gospel accounts of Jesus' miracles, one of the members broke in with a similar tone of protest, "How can you prove that?" Just about every truth claim we make, theological, philosophical or otherwise, carries with it certain underlying assumptions. If you carry those assumptions back far enough, you'll eventually get to the place where someone says without any sort of proof, "That's just the way things are." Wanting to know more about the assumptions behind his challenge, I asked a question, "Is your requirement of proof based upon a scientific viewpoint?" Getting only an evasive response, I pressed a bit further, "By that I mean, are you claiming we can't say anything is true or real unless it is supported by the scientific method?" This yielded a hesitant yes.

The requirement of proof is of course a valid stance in the realm of science. Those are the rules it lives by, confined to the observation and testing of the structure and workings of the natural world. But importing this standard into other aspects of life presents problems, problems which require further reflection. Prove it has become the unthinking mantra of secularism, possessing an allure of sorts, appearing to place the one asking for proof on a higher intellectual level. But in fact it avoids a deeper engagement with the world around us. For anyone with their eyes open and willing to look around, reality is complicated.

Still, in today's world, how can I object to this seemingly unassailable standard of scientific proof? I can because of three 'facts' which present themselves to us, each of them staring us in the face. All three are shrouded in complete mystery and will always remain so. They are realities which once engaged the greatest of thinkers, scientists, theologians and poets, but no longer. I'm speaking of the mystery of existence, the mystery of life and the mystery of human consciousness. Each of them poses an insurmountable counterweight to the words 'prove it.' But rather than engaging pseudoscience in a theological debate, let's put that aside. Instead let's challenge it upon its own terms, with the question of these three realities now turned upon pseudoscience, asking them to prove it.

Here We Are

Gazing into the star-filled sky has always been the supreme challenge to the mind. For centuries science was able to put these questions on the shelf by advancing the idea of an eternal and unchanging universe, saying in effect "It's always been there." The assumptions of this weak placeholder were shattered when Edwin Hubble looked into his telescope atop Mount Wilson observatory and made a few rough calculations. Until then it was thought our Milky Way encompassed everything, but Hubble realized that many of those small points of light weren't stars, they were other galaxies. Things suddenly got a whole lot bigger and a lot more complicated. His math yielded something else. These clusters of galaxies, far more vast in their distances than we ever thought, were moving apart from one another at incredible speeds. Hubble's discovery, together with the detection of the cosmic radiation background emanating from all directions of the cosmos, has led us to the Big Bang. There was a beginning and now we had to deal with it.

Science was suddenly presented with a metaphysical problem. Mystery now looked back at us. Confronted with a beginning, with creation, there had to be as Plato wrote a 'First mover,' or as Genesis proclaimed, "In the beginning." There is no scientific theory in which something comes from nothing. Such questions led scientists such as Robert Jastrow, former chief planetary scientist for NASA and also a former agnostic, to realize that everything had changed. He understood that creation needed a Creator.

The mystery only grew larger. With supercolliders hurling subatomic particles into one another at close to the speed of light, the hope is to discover in these collisions clues and artifacts of the Big Bang, what physics may have looked like at its inception. What they have learned is that the laws of physics we know today were all fixed within the first millionth of a second after the Big Bang. They've learned something else; all these laws were incredibly fined tuned for two things, for existence and for life. Astrophysicists have confirmed that the values of the four fundamental forces: gravity, electromagnetism, and the strong and weak nuclear forces, were determined in these initial nanoseconds. All the elemental forces of our universe possess very precise values, and if any of those values were to be altered, our universe would not exist.

If the ratio between the nuclear strong force and the electromagnetic force had been off by one part in 100,000,000,000,000,000, no stars would have formed. Neutrons are slightly heavier than protons with a ratio of masses of 939.56563 to 938.2723, very minor yet had it not been so, there would be no matter. The symbol E, used for the value of the forces holding atomic nuclei together is .00007. Had it been .00006 or .00008 there would be no atoms. If gravity was just slightly stronger, the universe would have collapsed upon itself long ago, slightly weaker then early gasses could not have coalesced into planets. These are just a few of the hundreds if not thousands of finely tuned forces. Change any of them, just slightly, and we aren't standing here.

Consider this analogy. You receive a large box of Legos in the mail, containing millions of pieces. Each one has a unique shape and in addition each one has one unique means of attaching itself to another. After some trial and error, you discover this pile of Legos constructs one thing and only one thing, say an elaborate castle. Would you then say, "What a coincidence," or would you conclude that some sort of order was imposed at the factory?

Science has put some math to the question of this exquisite order. What are the odds that all these properties, each one absolutely necessary for life and existence, would fall into these incredibly narrow ranges? Most calculations put the odds at ten to the sixtieth power. That's not a big number. It's an incomprehensible number, more than all the hydrogen molecules in our galaxy. This straightjacket was proving too tight for pseudoscience. Realizing it faced questions it could not answer, metaphysical questions, it responded with a theory worthy of being delivered by a leprechaun riding in on a unicorn, the multiverse theory. Acknowledging the incredible odds of such fine tuning, they came up with this idea: somehow trillions upon trillions of alternate universes are constantly bubbling up from what they call the Higgs field. In short, we just happened to get lucky, a jackpot far beyond all jackpots, far higher odds than every slot machine in Vegas coming up a winner at the same time, a million times over. Now you get a sense of how clever, and how unscientific, pseudoscience can be. There are no facts here, not even a coherent hypothetical equation. By the very nature of conjecturing an alternative universe, there is nothing we can observe, nothing which can ever be detected or tested.

Life

While watching the return of a popular science show on television, the moderator who is a noted scientist, opened the show by touting the rigors of science, how it relentlessly questions and examines everything. He then took the audience through a visual timeline of the earth's formation from early gases followed by its various stages until today. At one point, with active volcanoes and a swirling primordial atmosphere as his backdrop, he looked down at a pool of water and said, "Look down there, life is cooking."

This idea has common currency in many scientific circles, although they like to keep it vague. They speak in generalities, much like ancient alchemists, of water, heat and electricity thrown into a cauldron. Once mixed, here's how it works: life just popped up, abracadabra, that's it. An evolutionary biologist once wrote to the New York Times, urging scientist to stop talking about this, at least until we know something, anything. He was an agnostic and an honest one. Questions about the origin of life are at this point unknowable, and until even one piece of evidence pointing us in any direction is found, all should remain silent. Still, the question has to be directed at pseudoscience. Why would it advance an idea with no facts, no process and without a valid hypothesis? That question of course reflects motive and agenda rather than science.

Fully aware that it knows nothing about the origins of life, pseudoscience again reaches into its bag of tricks, throwing out what it hopes to be a trump card, yet more like a bluff. That card is time. If you just give our primordial soup enough time they say, well once again abracadabra. There is no known self-organizing life form. There is no process by which inorganic becomes organic. Time without an accompanying process is a meaningless scientific concept.

Still pseudoscience clings to its appeal of time, throwing out the analogy of a monkey at a typewriter, who will eventually over eons, type a word or a sentence. Their analogy breaks down quickly. First, they've assumed the monkey, a higher form of intelligence who can add information, but even if we grant pseudoscience their monkeys as well as the mechanism of a typewriter, how does an impersonal force go about building, shaping and creating? I might also add that an impersonal force can't possess accumulated knowledge. It would begin every day from zero trying to write its sentence.

That brings us to the word or sentence the monkey must type, in this case a single cell, since all life consists of cells as their basic building blocks. Each cell, and every cell which has ever existed, is incredibly and irreducibly complex. Each contains thousands of discrete biological machines with their own dedicated tasks. DNA sends information to form these machines, assimilating their hundreds of thousands of parts in a meticulous order. The millions of strands of DNA itself must be arranged in a precise manner; otherwise you don't have a cell. Our hypothetical monkeys, somehow feverishly at work every moment for billions of years, don't have to type a sentence. They would have to type every book in every library of the world, and even then they couldn't produce the complexity of a cell.

The Human Problem

There's another mystery science cannot account for, one you and I are familiar with. That's the mystery of human consciousness and creativity. Our minds process trillions of bits of information at close to the speed of light, but our experience tells us that we are more than just processors. We are self-aware, we love, we play and we pray. We find beauty and joy in art, in music and one another. None of this is the least bit necessary for survival in a Darwinist world. Yet pseudoscience is trying to convince us that our own life experience is a fiction. In their reductionist view, we're a complex compilation of biology and chemistry and nothing else.

Really, they've proved that? You've probably read the headlines; scientists have isolated in our brains the capacity for love or pinpointed our predispositions for altruism or religion. Our thoughts and our desires, they say, are generated by neurons and synapses. This may be the most malignant of all secular myths. When taught to a young college student, especially by people who are very smart, the effects of seeing ourselves as biological machines is life-defining. Such self-perception will determine how we go about the business of living, shaping all our values.

What's behind the sensational headlines claiming these scientific breakthroughs? Neuroscientists possess a powerful tool in what is called functional magnetic resonance imaging, or FMRI. Using its sensors and computers, likely you've seen its colorful crisscrossing brain maps displaying neural activity. But what are they really observing? We can see electrical activity, and we can see certain portions of the brain suddenly using more oxygen, but what does that tell us? Observing doesn't necessarily mean understanding. Yet this hasn't stopped some neuroscientists from pointing to one of these lines of their brain maps and exclaiming, "Look here is the genesis of an idea."

It's always helpful to take a step back, especially from something so impressive, and ask a few common sense questions. If we expose someone to fear or anxiety for example, and a part of the brain then lights up, is that a breakthrough? To say the external world can trigger an internal physical reaction is something all of us already know. Also, can't anyone see that this is the ultimate chicken and egg problem, likely one never to be solved? Does the neuron produce the thought, an odd concept for a group of cells, or does the thought produce the electrical impulse? If we place two subjects, say Mozart and a shoe repairman, under an FRMI and observe similar neural pathways, what should be conclude? Are they both composing a symphony or are they both repairing shoes?

Creativity

Pseudoscience is confronted with an even more daunting human problem in its characterization of man as machine, the problem of creativity. Neuroscientists like to compare our brains to computers, an analogy now under assault by an increasing number of scientists who say we simply don't work that way. Even so, computers don't create. They can spit out binary ones and zeroes, using patterns given to them by their programmers, then translating those ones and zeroes into our language or number system. Sometimes they can spit out patterns we didn't expect, but the rules they work by are those given to them. In this way computers can mimic thinking and creativity, but they cannot create in the human sense. Unlike us they can't conceive of something outside of their programming.

Creativity presents a nagging issue for pseudoscience. How can it explain someone such as Einstein who, with his theories of relativity, was able to see the world in a completely new way? Time and space as no longer fixed but something malleable, defying all perception and intuition. How do we explain composers, poets and artists? How do we explain ourselves? Even some secularists are beginning to push back on the human computer metaphor as one too sterile and too limited in describing our experience. But militant atheists such as Sam Harris or David Dawkins respond with their elevated rhetoric, describing our biological machines as things of wonder which evoke beauty and awe. Their words however betray them. Of what use is awe, or a sense of beauty, in their deterministic world of Darwinism. Of what evolutionary use is wonder? Can we take a supercomputer and place it in front of a Renoir or a Matisse and ask of it, do you think this is beautiful? We await an answer.

Separate Realms.

All this may leave us asking, who cares? Can't Christians hold fast to their faith and let science do its thing? It is the nature of worldviews to compete for supremacy. Rarely can they co-exist without one claiming their truth is greater than another's. Once religion had crossed over into the boundaries of science, now science has invaded the boundaries of faith. Pseudoscientific claims are persuasive, often they sound compelling, primarily because science has achieved so much. It has extended our lives and peered into deep space. It's so impressive it's hard to argue with. But the tacit lie of pseudoscience is this: because science has solved so many of our problems, one day it will solve all our problems. There is no logical necessity to such a stance. Newton was considered the last word on physics until Einstein demonstrated his theories of motion and gravity were incomplete. Later Einstein's own findings were rendered incomplete by quantum mechanics. Each discovery opens a new door into a new vista, but that vista always presents new unopened doors.

Add to all this the new scientist who has become the celebrity, with bestselling books and their own television shows. The temptation is to entertain and dazzle rather than confining themselves to the rigors of science. They know book sales and ratings will plunge if they stay within the boundaries of science and acknowledge, "For now the evidence is inconclusive."

Decades ago the eminent psychiatrist Carl Jung foresaw a new man entranced by technology and science. He predicted a new world which would attempt to define itself by reason, abandoning our spiritual side. Jung also saw the consequences. This new man he said would not evolve to higher and higher levels of reason. With religion lost, man's innate need for meaning and transcendence would instead lead him towards the occult and fantasy as his only coping mechanisms. How else do we account for the proliferation of Armageddon scenarios, apocalypse and the other mythical stories we see today? Is our explosion of fantasy and mythmaking a reflection of a soulless man's search for his soul? Can it be that people find life today so sterile and so unsatisfying, these fantasies have become our poor substitutes?

Now Prove It

Let's return to the young divinity student who challenged the professor of religion with her objection of 'prove it.' He thought for a moment and met her challenge with one of his own, "Is that really the right question?" Pausing for a moment to extend his answer he said, "Take all the people in your life who have influenced you, who have nurtured and mentored you, making you the person you are today. Now prove it." This is the challenge our modern world cannot meet. The words 'prove it' lie only on the surface of things. Think of your own loved ones, friends and family, those who have shaped you as uniquely you by their love and devotion. Tell me that all their love and their self-giving can be reduced to electrical impulses.

Chapter Seven

Messages of Modernity

2 Corinthians 11:14 Even Satan disguises himself as an angel of light. So it is not strange if his ministers also disguise themselves as ministers of righteousness.

We've already seen several ways in which our new culture transmits its values, whether though its elevated rhetoric, catchphrases or pseudoscience passing itself off as science. From art, to mass media, to technology, there are hundreds if not thousands of secular messages expressing and reinforcing the Post-Christian revolution. Much like the mythical Greek character Narcissus, who endlessly gazed at his own reflection in a pond, our modern messages reflect an uncritical and unthinking affirmation of modern man, an inflated self without boundaries. This chapter takes a look at a few of these cultural voices by asking an embarrassing question. Where are today's great works of art rivaling Rembrandt or Matisse? Who are the great writers of today we can compare to Homer, Shakespeare or Tolstoy to name a few? Why is classical music something we retrieve only from our distant past? In our self-declared sophistication, why can't we create our own masterpieces?

Art and Literature

While waiting for a public lecture to begin at a local university, I noticed a small art exhibit at the far end of the concourse. With a few minutes to kill I walked over to take a look. What I observed was a single work, a multi-colored paper Mache shark lying on the floor with a stream of household garbage streaming from its mouth. Seated nearby was a young college student, who I assumed to be the artist. After a few minutes of reflection I asked her a question, "Can you please tell me your interpretation of your work?" Anticipating something along the lines of an artistic protest against pollution in the oceans, I was somewhat surprised by her reply, "I really don't have one. I'm hoping an observer will project their own meaning upon the art."

Her reply told me a lot, not only about the state of today's art, but about many of our modern messages. Her art wasn't intended to convey any intrinsic truth; in fact it wasn't intended to convey anything. In a sense both the art and the artist were absent, asking the audience to imbue the work with its meaning. The art was whatever we wanted it to be, our narcissistic reflection. Her comments caused me later to reflect upon tours I took to the Vatican and the Louvre, as the guide led us through the art and architecture, pointing out its imbedded and hidden treasures, the use of proportion, small gestures on the canvas or sculpture, minor details which evoked moments in history, brushstrokes, their use of geometry and the like. The guides brought out not only the beauty of the art but its story as well. Art once made statements, not so much about the artist, but about the great themes of life, either religious or reflections upon the human drama. Great art was once didactic, causing us to reflect upon both the great heights and the great tragedies of man. We were moved to think about the shared struggle of life and the spirit of overcoming. Art asked our minds to reach.

Now we are left with Andy Warhol's soup cans or a Jackson Pollack's canvas with paint flung upon it in wild random gestures.

They may have been expressing themselves, but who knows since their abstractions are unmoored to culture or history. There's no story, and a culture without story is aimless and without a future.

Literature has for the most part traveled down the same road. Much of our fiction today consists of the author's self-reflection, a personal experience unconnected to anything higher or universal. This is the return to Descartes, where nothing apart from our own minds can inform us. The great tradition of Western writers from Chaucer, Dickens, Faulkner and many others, presented to us the complexities of the human condition, matters shared in our quest for such things as courage or redemption. They reflected a journey shared, rather than a solitary road of the self.

Like so many other things from our past, the study of classical Western literature is on the wane. Faculty and students alike dismiss the classics rather than honestly engaging them, using shorthand labels to condemn the writers for living in a male-centric world or one which gave no voice to minorities. Such criticism is revealing. How can they peer so clearly into the author's mind, reducing great writing to their own political agendas? How can we ask of these authors the impossible, requiring them to somehow leap out of their own time and milieu? This reflects the triumphalism of now which relegates the past to irrelevance. The study of literature should in fact be more diverse, but that isn't what the critics are asking. Their attacks reveal a power grab because they advocate exclusion prior to any new inclusion. Perhaps the wisdom of the past, with its assertions of objective truths, poses a threat.

Forgotten in this controversy is the goal of great literature, meant to speak beyond the ages and addressed to all people. George Orwell wants us to see the subtleties of totalitarianism before it is too late. In Macbeth, Shakespeare wants to tell us something about the destructiveness of revenge. Homer's Iliad shows us a world which venerates its heroes in battle, but with the petulant Achilles and the stench of death, we're forced to reflect more deeply about war's true cost. Classical Western literature urged upon us a greater sense of self-understanding and self-reflection. We learn our most profound lessons from others, especially from the gifted artist or writer, deeper lessons we cannot glean from our often jaded personal reflections. Does modern man not share with the man of the past such things as ego, jealousy and love? Over time has the spectrum of human hope and desire really changed?

Advertising

While watching college football all day, I began to notice something about the commercials, especially the car ads. None of them actually sold the car. There was little mention of performance. Such things as the transmission, handling or reliability were rarely mentioned. In one ad a sexy woman caressed the stick shift, extolling the car's rumbling horsepower with a sensuous tone. In another a sophisticated handsome looking man drove his sports car down the street, in slow motion, basking in the admiration of onlookers. They weren't selling cars. They were selling sex, success or self-esteem. A few other car ads depicted the perfect family on a camping trip with the sun always shining, beautiful people and all smiles. They were selling us a lifestyle, absent our imperfections and our dysfunctional families.

I began to notice other ads, one for eyeglasses which promised you would come out of the store as a 'new you.' A resort commercial said you would discover your 'real life.' A soft drink ad promised a similar evolution with a teenager dancing down the street wearing a T-shirt proclaiming her as 'one of a kind,' followed by the irony of hundreds of others joining in, all with the same message on their T-shirts.

I shared my observations with a friend who owns a small public relations firm. He immediately responded, "Of course, you never sell the product." What they're selling is a new life and unfulfilled dreams. This of course assumes a deep dissatisfaction with your present life, along with the odd idea that toothpaste or perfume can give us what we want. My friend suggested that I get on the internet and look at some old commercials from the 1960s. They were very different, they too had a little glitz and glamour, but the spokesperson talked about the performance and styling of the car, or the medicine's positive effects. They were actually selling the product.

The advertising industry spends billions of dollars not just on media but psychology, plotting our eye movements, picking the brains of focus groups, probing our conscious and subconscious. Their goal is to create a strong emotional connection between you and the product. Bound up in this premise is our suspension of rationality, which leads us to another embarrassing question directed towards modernity. Why are we so seduced? Why does this new man, believing he is guided by science and reason, place his hopes and identity upon deodorant and beer?

Technology

In any discussion about the profusion of modern messages, the internet comes to mind with its billions of daily hits, tweets, shares and likes. Like many of our other modern miracles, technology comes with a dark side, not just the cyber bullying and access to pornography, but the technology itself. As the communications expert Marshall McLuhan once wrote, "The medium is the message." The sheer scope and speed of the internet carries with it a seduction, a small device we can hold in our hand, serving as a portal to an endless array of news, products, feelings, opinions and people. Its immediacy constantly impinges upon our world, leaving little attention for anything else. Graphics are so dazzling that we refer to them as virtual reality. Even when logged off, it beckons us back, off line we feel as if we have been cast off the world.

Psychological studies are just now assessing the human cost of our technology. Not only a cognitive cost but an emotional one as well. Nicholas Carr's bestseller, "The Shallows: What the Internet

Is Doing to Our Brains," chronicles in detail the damaging effects. Our focus is diminished, with the constant streaming of information leaving us no time for reflection. With books our minds are allowed to create images, while the cyber world supplies them for us, diminishing our imaginations.

All of this cannot but help but spill out into our relational world. When I watch people standing in a crowd staring into their smart phones, we are at the same time together and alone. Real communication requires a voice, touch, a face and gestures. Increasingly we have hundreds of virtual friends, but no one to whom we can turn to for real intimacy. We share trivialities but little of our real selves. We chat with someone on the other side of the globe, hardly knowing our next door neighbor. Even what we do reveal on social media is a fictional person up for sale. The staggering statistics tells us we are living in an epidemic of loneliness and isolation, with the cost of technology nothing less than our humanity. We are relational beings, it's who we are. Is this what we call connectivity?

Death

Genesis 3:4 But the serpent said to the woman, "You will not die."

What does death reveal about us? According to our messages, they say quite a lot. Watching a series of television commercials sponsored by a funeral home chain, I noticed something odd. The sales pitch wasn't directed so much at the bereaved family, but to the person about to die. It said you could have your own personalized funeral, a ceremony all about you. One showed a boat atop the casket as pallbearers lifted oars towards the sky in a final salute to a rowing enthusiast. In another commercial jars of the deceased's famous barbecue sauce were handed out to everyone, the secret recipe finally revealed. Each of them had a party atmosphere, sunshine radiated and people smiled in synch with the upbeat pop music.

Of course we should celebrate the life of the deceased. We should gather and tell the stories of how much they meant to us. But something looms over what we call our celebrations of life and that's death. All our infused inspiration, our eulogies about someone who lived their life to the fullest, can't negate the dark reality. Death's eternal consequences still confront us. Perhaps another story should be told.

The funeral services I've attended recently seem to be sharing the same script as the television commercials. Eulogies are filled with euphemisms, my favorite, "He will live on in the memories of others." I want to jump up and say, no he won't, and even if we entertained this fantasy, all the 'others' will eventually die as well. Today's funerals have become yet another reflection of a culture unmoored from its faith. Unable to face death, we now engage in elaborate rituals of avoidance. Do we really think our eloquence and our celebrations have any power over the grave? Perhaps in our world without the transcendent, that's all we have left.

A recent television documentary on teen suicide featured a California high school, chosen because its suicide rate exceeded the now unprecedented national level. Counterintuitive was the fact that the school wasn't located in the inner city. Just the opposite, it was located in one of the state's most affluent counties near a prestigious university. Most of the kids were from stable families, with a disproportionate number of parents either professors or working in Silicon Valley. Everything about the place was exceptional from academic awards to Ivy League placements. They were our future elites, living in a world of privilege and plenty, but according to the statistics it was also a world of unease and alienation. High school life was wrapped up in achievement, getting into the right schools so they could land the right career. Problem was, that appeared to be it.

Interviews of the students and psychologists revealed something else. None of them was able to venture a reason for the school's overwhelming number of suicides. The choice of bright well-off students taking their lives was to each of them an impenetrable puzzle. A few talked about academic pressures in a more competitive world, but pressure is everywhere. Besides, their explanations were for me somewhat muted after hearing my father's stories of growing up in the Depression. Talking about pressure or fitting in, spoke more about our modern fragility than anything else.

The psychologists were armed with reams of data but little else. The secular world, one which had reduced us to soulless creatures, was unable to articulate anything which reached into the human heart. Depression was described as a disease, and it is, but there was no discussion of the anxious and unstable world which can give rise to our depression. Addiction was also termed a disease, rightly so, as the social scientists called for more treatment centers, yet absent any understanding of the emotional and spiritual deficits which lead a person to reach for drugs in the first place. A world of scientific reductionism, absent the human spirit, left them only to wonder.

One of the students interviewed, recalled a friend who stood on the nearby tracks of a high speed train, she too was unable to summon anything of the interior. Questions of death lapsed into tests, college applications, the stresses of dating and her high school software development project. Then she added almost as an afterthought, "One day we will overcome death." Hers was a modern day statement of faith. Her highest hopes, her way out of a gray world, somehow rested in technology. It said in effect, we will find a way to save ourselves while her prediction carried with it an irony. Living in a world of silent despair, her only hope was simply to extend it.

Her faith statement wasn't just a teenage fantasy. Her confidence is shared by many under the banner of the Trans humanist movement. It's not a fringe group, with experts such as Ray Kurzweil, director of engineering for Google, writing several bestsellers on the subject. The movement has already received funding in the hundreds of millions of Silicon Valley dollars, and according to these futurists, hope is just around the corner. They claim that advances in gene therapy and nanotechnology will soon allow humans to live forever. Kurzweil says one day we will be able to download our consciousness into computers. Brilliant women and men don't always make wise ones, nor does their brilliance always illuminate them of their limitations. Trans humanism is just another Tower of Babel, our prideful projects attempting to reach towards the heavens and escape our finitude in man's unending attempt to blur the line between God and man, heaven and earth. Downloading ourselves to a computer also reveals our modern self-image, one without any spirit. It says we can be reduced to algorhythms.

The Other Story

The other story we should by telling at funerals isn't about us. In Church we tell a story of a God who entered our world and took upon himself our human skin, suffering death and overcoming it for our sake. Rather than stories recounting the deceased's hobbies, this story doesn't need any rhetoric or flights of fantasy because it deals with a real hope. Christians can boldly stare directly into the darkness and say "Death, where is thy sting?" In this acknowledgement of our inability to save ourselves, we tell a love story of a God who died and descended into hell so we don't have to. This is also a story of gratitude. For Christians, this place and this moment of death, is precisely where we declare victory, not ours but God's.

These are only a few of our messages, reflecting back to us a distorted image of ourselves. From art to advertising to technology, we should step back from this reflection, realizing it can be easily destroyed simply by tossing a small pebble into our waters. When the prophets of modernity preach their better world with all their metrics and data, we can look around and see for ourselves that their spiritless world is beginning to fall apart. The soulless man, no longer anchored in tradition or faith, is a doomed experiment. The elites are helpless to explain the massive increase in the use of antidepressants, suicide rates at their highest levels ever, an epidemic of addictions, the disintegration of the middle class and hundreds of other failed metrics because they lack a human face. They have the data but they have no answers. For Christians, we've been given something of a measuring rod to assess our world around us. We are told to judge the tree by the fruit it bears.

Chapter Eight

Within The Walls

2 Peter 2:1 But false prophets also arose among the people, just as there will be false teachers among you, who will secretly bring in destructive opinions.

Now that we've seen how the secular world advances its belief system, whether in the political or academic arenas, here we will see how its energies are often directed at the Church. In fact this is where it often expends its greatest efforts.

In the Grand Miracle, C.S. Lewis writes about this secular intrusion into the Church, describing in his time a new kind of clergy who rejects Christian orthodoxy. Lewis cites their oft-given defense, "We came about our new ideas honestly," but that's not the point he says. All of us think our ideas are honestly held. The point, according to Lewis, is a minister of the Gospel who doesn't believe in the Gospel, as he offers an analogy of a conservative who later becomes a Communist. It may have been an honest change of heart, but to remain in the conservative party while espousing Communism isn't just a case of intellectual dishonesty, it's tantamount to a foreign agent working within.

The struggle to hold back cultural compromise isn't something new to the Christian Church. The letters of Apostle Paul confronted a host of first century challenges he described as the "god of this age." In his first letter to the Corinthians, the threat came in the form of Greeks who brought to the Church some of their classical philosophical baggage. Likely they were of the Stoic school in the tradition of Plato, believing the path to salvation was only for an elite few who were able to cultivate a higher form of wisdom. In their attempt to fuse Greek philosophy with Christ, Paul unequivocally said no. He recognized the threat they posed to the Gospel, again it was man saving man though his own efforts. According to Paul salvation was the free and gracious act of God alone beyond our human endeavors, "God's act is foolishness to the perishing, but to us saved, it is the power of God." Paul would make no compromises, "Jews demand signs. Greeks desire wisdom but we preach Christ crucified."

In Galatia Paul dealt with another challenge, this time a group of Jewish converts who claimed circumcision was necessary for salvation. Beyond its obvious legalisms, Paul saw the deeper existential threat to the Church. Requiring circumcision implicitly said that the death and resurrection of Christ was not the final and decisive act of our salvation. Circumcision meant something more was needed, and that something more was to be supplied by us. In the face of this constant cultural refrain, Paul possessed the clarity needed for today's Church. He understood that the insertion of any human agency into God's decisive act upon the cross would rob the Gospel of its grace and power, a cancer which would eventually grow.

Trying to build a Church from the ground up, preaching the most unlikely and paradoxical message ever proclaimed, while trying to counter the torrent of Roman power, Paul was likely tempted to embrace the big tent approach. The temptation to be inclusive, welcoming all sorts of other beliefs and cultural views into a fusion with Christ, would have been strong. What harm could it be to include a little Greek philosophy? What's the downside in allowing a circumcision sect to do their own thing, especially since Jesus himself was circumcised? In his letter to the Galatians, Paul soundly rejected any such synchronism, "The Gospel is not of human origin." When we ask in our own time how the Church should respond to all the outside influences posed by modernity, Paul's vision of the Church should be our guide. In defense of the Gospel, given by God and not man, Paul was zealous in resisting any compromise with a pluralistic world, "If any man preaches any other Gospel to you other than that received, let him be accursed." The Pauline letters were included in the Bible for many reasons, one of them I'm sure was to serve as guidance for the Church through the ages. All people are invited into the Church, but not all beliefs. It is a Church universal, yet it stands for not just a mishmash of worldly ideas but one eternal and unchanging truth claim of a divine Christ who has reconciled the world to himself. "I am the Truth," he said, and this truth was spelled with a capital T.

The Frontal Assault: The Creeds.

Creeds are the means by which the Church guards against these dangerous compromises with the outside world. By stating our core beliefs, successive generations take an uncompromising stand. Simply put, we say this is true, and for that reason it's not surprising that the modern cultural assault often begins here. Standing together and reciting the creeds, Christians proclaim the most profound thing any person can ever say, "I believe." Not how we feel or what people generally think, but a belief in something external and eternal. We declare an objective reality beyond ourselves, declaring openly a Creator who made us, a God who came into our world and a God who died for our sake.

The Nicene Creed

I believe in one God, the Father Almighty.
Maker of heaven and earth, and of all things visible and invisible.
I believe in one Lord Jesus Christ, the only begotten Son of God,
God from God, Light from Light,

> True God from true God, begotten not made, being of one substance with the Father;
> Through him all things were made.
> For us and for our salvation, he came down from heaven,
> And by the Holy Spirit was incarnate of the Virgin Mary and became man.
> For our sake he was crucified under Pontius Pilate, he suffered death and was buried,
> And he rose again on the third day in accordance with the Scriptures.
> He ascended into heaven and is seated at the right hand of the Father.
> He will come again in glory to judge the living and the dead,
> And his kingdom will have no end.
> I believe in the Holy Spirit, the Lord, the giver of life,
> Who proceeds from the Father and the Son,
> Who with the Father and the Son is worshipped and glorified,
> Who has spoken through the prophets.
> I believe in one, holy, catholic and apostolic Church,
> I confess one baptism for the forgiveness of sins
> And I look for the resurrection of the dead and the life of the world to come. Amen

With the activist bent C.S. Lewis describes, secularism has set its sights on the creeds, branding statements of 'I believe' as a form of propaganda or an infringement upon our free thinking. A sampling of quotes below from an article written by an Episcopal priest entitled, "To Creed or Not to Creed," openly questioning whether his congregation should recite the Nicene Creed, tells us a great deal about modern tactics and their aims.

"Anyone who's ever been to a Roman Catholic mass or Holy Eucharist at the Episcopal Church will recognize these familiar lines from the Nicene Creed. Most people take it for granted, part of the Christian package deal because in any package deal there's always something you don't want or can't use, so the creed often ends up in the intellectual trash can."

Something we can retrieve from the trash can is this minister's unsubstantiated claim that most of us don't take the creed seriously. How does he take such license to speak for millions who recite it every Sunday, saying 'I believe,' telling us from his privileged position that we don't really believe? Another item to be plucked from the dumpster is his assumption that the Nicene Creed is nothing more than a package deal. This is a clever rhetorical trick intended to appeal to the modern mindset by recasting the creed as simply a mishmash of ideas, rather than a succinct and time-worn statement of core beliefs. Here he panders to the postmodernist, where the individual is in charge, deciding what they like and don't like, what is worthy of our allegiance and what is not. According to this priest, packages are somehow by their nature, pernicious forms of indoctrination, but Christian orthodoxy, especially the creeds, weren't formulated simply for the sake of conformity. It's a stripped-down assertion that certain basic things in life are true. In our freedom we can accept or reject, but creeds don't allow us to pick and choose or rewrite it in our own fashion. Our personal preferences don't make the creeds any less true. How far we have fallen when a two thousand year old statement, concerning our origin and destiny, is to us so tenuous and so irrelevant, that we can say of these life-determining statements, "It's something I don't want or I can't use."

"When I began examining the creeds from an intellectual perspective, I came smack up against the wall of a stark reality, these things aren't literally true. Asked by my parishioners and seekers, 'Do you believe in the creed father?' My response is this: I read the Nicene Creed as a historic document but understand it as a metaphor."

His sweeping claim that the Nicene Creed can't be true from an intellectual standpoint lacks any intellectual rigor whatsoever, just his personal opinion without bothering to engage any of the creed's truth claims. Likely his statement that "it can't be true," rests upon a pseudoscientific worldview which we encountered in an earlier chapter, one we found dubious in the face of our own experience. We can also ask of this priest: how can he stand before his congregation and speak to them about anything spiritual while residing in his Enlightenment pseudoscientific world, unable to reach further than the constructions of our own minds?

The Gospel writers knew some science. They were fully aware that dead bodies don't get up and walk out of a tomb three days later. Their claim of a resurrection was just as astounding and countercultural in the first century as it is today. That's why the Gospels describe the crucifixion and resurrection stories with very little symbolism, recounting it in stark matter of fact terms. They emphasize a resurrected Jesus appearing, touching, eating and speaking, all in order to say the resurrection wasn't an idea or dream, but something they experienced. It was paradoxical to all human thought, then and now, written not from the stance of a philosopher or mystic, instead they called themselves witnesses.

The priest's characterization of the creed as only metaphor reveals an agenda of prior doubt, unwilling to probe and investigate its claims. He's willing to mouth the words, yet he lacks the courage to stand in front of the cross and say, 'It's only a symbol, it didn't happen and I don't believe.' Instead, he reflects a secularism which seeks comfort by rewriting it for each individual, the Enlightenment project of reconstructing our own reality. Metaphor is, of course, necessary to any religious expression. We're trying to say something of the transcendent, something beyond, yet with our earthly language. We're trying to express what can't be fully expressed. Oddly the secular world will embrace the metaphors of poets and writers, even those of the occult and fantastic, yet any symbolism of the Bible is dismissed in a shorthand manner.

Lost in his criticism is the fact that the Nicene Creed has little in the way of symbolic statements. At the heart of the creed is a declaration that 'this happened.' We say God made the world. We say Jesus was born of a woman, who had a name Mary. We say Jesus suffered and died, adding a reference to Pontius Pilate to affirm its historicity. The creed is a statement of what God has already done, in time and history, yet at the same time in its divine power and mystery, constitutes events which transcend time and history.

His broad brush, relegating the creed to mere metaphor, casts another malignant seed. Perhaps secular humanism intuitively knows something. If they can sell us a statement which only pretends to say I believe, relegating matters of life and death to the purely symbolic, then the creed will forever remain for us at arms-length. People will not stake their lives upon metaphors. Symbolism will never claim our hearts. Before the first word, modernity is closed off from the creed's story, a love story of a God who had no need to create, yet does so because he desires an object of his love. It's a story of a God who gave himself to a lost world, simply because he wanted it back in his embrace. Maybe in some recess, the secular world knows if mankind ever opened its heart to this story, we would be bound to this God forever.

"At the Council of Nicaea in 325 C.E., bickering bishops gathered to settle once and for all the question of Jesus' humanity versus his divinity. At the time Jesus was considered Son of God and an extraordinary human being but not part of the Godhead. The Nicene Creed, a compromise creed, was first accepted at the Council of Nicaea but then rejected only to be reinstituted by a later council in Constantinople in 381, which is when Jesus finally and officially became God."

Our priest is hoping you don't know much history, especially Church history. If you do, you will immediately realize that he gets only one fact right, the Council of Nicaea did meet in 325 A.D. Describing the council as a group of bickering bishops who hammered out some sort of political compromise, is at best disingenuous. Historians have access to many sources, including the actual record of proceedings at Nicaea, which reveals a very different story beginning with a priest named Arius from Alexandria. Arius claimed Jesus was created by God and therefore not God's co-equal. Because this was considered heresy at the time, a group of bishops appealed to the Roman Emperor Constantine to convene a council. More than three hundred bishops from as far as Britain and North Africa met for over a month, debating Scripture and Church teaching. A very small group who initially were willing to entertain Arius' position soon came down on the side of the Church. When a vote was finally taken, Arius was rejected by a margin of 316 to 2. So this is what our priest characterizes as a 'compromise?' As far as his other claim, that Jesus finally and officially became God only in 381, he's also hoping you don't read the Bible, especially the first chapter of the Gospel of John in his description of Jesus as the Logos or Word. "In the beginning was the Word, and the Word was with God, and the Word was God."

"I keep coming back to my belief that the creed has outlived its usefulness and we probably don't need it at all. In essence the creed symbolizes the reluctance of the church to acknowledge the times we live in. Should a new creed be written, or should a personal creed, said silently, be substituted during mass?"

By declaring the creed as an out of date liability, he announces a new creed of modernity, born of individualism handed down from our Enlightenment and drawn deeper into the narcissism of postmodernism. God now needs to be updated so he can get with the times. Not only does his new creed fail to see God as God, but it also fails to see man as man. What of the human condition, of our deepest longings, has changed and needs updating? The technological furniture surrounding us has changed but has the human heart? We're still born in an unknowable universe, and with each breath we take we're drawn closer and closer towards the mystery of death.

All men and women, throughout all times, have shared the same anxieties, the same fears and the same hopes. We are ourselves grand mysteries, who should be astonished we are here, thinking, loving and desiring. What of this needs updating? Will this new personal creed show us the way in the face of such questions?

In its attempt to cast the creed as shackles upon our freedoms, secularism fastens its own chains and imposes its own form of indoctrination. The Church doesn't ask for unthinking followers. Its teachings, doctrines and creeds are ways of asking us to think more deeply, to consider the meaning of a world outside of ourselves. The creeds proclaim we are uniquely made and uniquely loved and in response it asks us to turn towards our Creator and say something profoundly human, "I believe."

The Back Door: Social Justice

Not all threats to the Church are as obvious and direct as those aimed at the creeds. Some assaults even appear benign, borrowing their roots from Christian tradition. One of those comes in the form of the Church's social justice movement.

Oliver Wendell Holmes once wrote, "There are certain phrases which only serve as an excuse for not thinking." A few years back, as I was listening to a sermon, the Supreme Court Justice's words came back to me. The minister was telling the congregation how it should feel about a host of social issues from open immigration to universal health care. It was worth hearing, especially for an upper middle class audience, but in closing he told us why we should get on board with his programs, "Because God is love." You can see the power of a phrase as a substitute for thinking, especially one as true as this.

Do we always know where God's love is directing us? In a complicated world, with competing views on all sides, can we easily claim God's love for our side? Without the discernment of prayer and

Scripture, often we find that our claims are really in fact projections upon God of our own agendas.

In using the term social justice, I'm referring to a movement within the Church which gives priority to social issues of the day, whether race, income equality, sexuality or the like. The trend is not just within the Church but can also be found in many divinity schools, where a curriculum of theology has given way to sociology. Questions of social justice have always been at the forefront of the Church's mission, and when they haven't, the Church has failed itself. Social justice runs throughout the Old Testament, spoken by prophets to an often wayward Israel who worshipped in the Temple but neglected the widow and orphan. The Jesus we encounter in the New Testament has a special empathy for the poor and downtrodden. The question then for the Church is not whether it should be promoting social justice, but rather one of priority and emphasis. Looking beyond the nice sounding catchphrases, first we need to ask several questions of the social justice movement: When does the call for social justice become a disguise for politics? If social justice becomes our priority, will the Church lose its identity as the Body of Christ? Finally, isn't justice often in the eye of the beholder?

With respect to the last question, justice can be complicated, although today it's often presented to us as a matter already settled. If unbridled immigration should cost someone their job, do we go to them and say, "That's justice." If free healthcare drains the treasury's resources away from other worthy programs, do we say to those who lose out, "That's justice."

What is the answer and what should be our priority? A prior question presents itself: where does the Church go to find answers to these questions? History shows the Church has often lost its footing, but it has always regained it, not only surviving but eventually thriving. The Church has always found its place to stand in difficult times by asking one question: what does the life of Christ, as revealed in Scripture, say to us?

Turning to the Bible, we notice that Jesus never identifies with any particular group or cause, not even one of the Jewish sects of his time. There were no demands to overthrow the current political or economic order, although certainly he expected the Church to carry out his unfinished business. Still, in first century Palestine, a place of abject poverty and oppression, where women were at best second class citizens, something confronts us. Jesus never explicitly takes on the Roman Empire. There's nothing about women's rights. He doesn't even mention the scourge of slavery. Of course he cared about such matters passionately, but his silence may give us some much needed perspective.

Was social justice left to the Church? In many ways it was. In the Book of Acts we find the early Church going about the business of caring for widows and orphans, countercultural to a Greco-Roman world which had no sense of institutional charity. Tertullian wrote of the first century pagan astonishment as they observed these new Christian communities, "Look how they love one another!"

But the priority is found in Christ's great commission. Jesus didn't tell his disciples to fight for their rights. He told them to "Go and make disciples of all nations, baptizing in the name of the Father, Son and Holy Spirit." The question of priority is also addressed in an interesting story found in the sixth chapter of the Book of Acts. There we find Church leadership overwhelmed by the needs of the poor, forcing the disciples to meet and ask, "Is it not right to neglect the word of God and wait on tables?" In answering the question of priority, they delegated these charitable duties to a group called deacons, enabling the disciples to once again take up their commission.

Matthew's Sermon on the Mount may also tell us something about social justice. One of the central themes in his Gospel is the kingdom of God. John the Baptist's first words are "Repent for the kingdom of God is near," and later when Jesus begins his public ministry, he utters the same words, "Repent for the kingdom of God is near." Matthew knows his readers have some questions. What does this kingdom look like? How do I become a part of it? Much of the Sermon on the Mount is an exposition of these questions, as Jesus presents an upside down kingdom counterintuitive to the world's ways. "Blessed are the poor in spirit, theirs is the kingdom. The meek shall inherit the earth. If a solider impresses you into service for one mile, you go two." He says we should "not resist and evildoer." Here we notice something about the kingdom and about following Christ. No one here is crying out for their rights. No one slapped in the face asks for recourse. No one, whose shirt is taken, cries out for reparations. It tells us that something far greater than our notions of social justice is at work in this kingdom.

Jesus enjoins his disciples to begin living in this kingdom, free from the world's snatching and grabbing ways, free from retaliation and anger, even renouncing our status as victims. The world's power move against Christians isn't met with our own power move. How often in the course of history have we seen the oppressed rise up, only to become the oppressor? This does not suggest a Jesus who is indifferent or passive in the face of injustice. He calls out the Pharisees as they pass by the poor in their lavish robes. He calls out the royal privilege of King Herod and drives the moneychangers from the Temple. Still, Jesus leaves all these powers in place, at least for now. But why?

The far deeper story is to be found in the story of Christ's crucifixion. Why would the Roman Empire expend such efforts to put to death an itinerant preacher without an army? Why would an entrenched priestly order care about one man with a ragtag group of followers? What would drive the crowd to their frenzied shouts of 'crucify him,' when Jesus only healed the sick and preached hope? In each of the Gospels an indictment is leveled against everyone, the government, the religious institutions and we the people so easily swayed. It's as if all the powers and institutions of this world knew in some deep recess that the proclamation of God's impending kingdom necessarily meant the overthrow of all our own kingdoms.

This is the sense in which Jesus is radical beyond all our concepts of radicalism. History shows us that all sides have attempted to enlist Jesus for their own cause, yet none of them understands that his kingdom is so revolutionary and so encompassing, all our human agendas will fall on their knees. This is what Jesus meant when he said you can't put new wine into old wineskins or sew a new patch of cloth on an old coat. The new will burst forth, destroying the old. The new world will literally tear the old world asunder.

The Church also faces another difficult question, one often posed by a secular culture. Can Christianity claim that its efforts for justice are any different than those of any other relief agency? Christians should support other charitable works undertaken by the world. The Bible is filled with examples of God using unbelievers to carry out his purposes. But if we cannot lay claim to a difference, we have to ask whether there any justification for the Church.

What is this difference? For one it is the promise of empowerment. In Jesus' farewell discourse to his disciples in the closing chapters of the Gospel of John, he tells them he will return in the form of the Holy Spirit, using the imagery of a vine and branches, "I am the vine, you are the branches. Those who abide in me and I in them bear much fruit, because apart from me you can do nothing." Showing them other side of the coin he says, "With me you can do anything." Given this promise, why would Christians not so dedicate all their efforts?

The story of Jesus' temptation in the desert tells us something else about this difference. Satan's command to Jesus, to turn stones into bread, on its face doesn't appear to be something wrong. In fact by using his power to make bread out of stones, Jesus could feed the world. But in his rejection of Satan's temptation, "Man does not live by bread alone but by the word of God," we realize that Christ comes for a greater purpose. Humanity has a far deeper hunger than bread can ever satisfy. This is the point of departure of Christian justice and its worldly counterpart. It isn't that the efforts of the world are wrong or even misguided. The problem exists in the fact that they aim so low.

Returning to the question as to why Jesus didn't start the anti-Rome party or the anti-slavery movement, there is no simple answer. But in any fair reading of the Gospels, it is apparent Jesus wasn't as concerned about reforming the world as he was in transforming it. Far beyond the issues of our political or economic orders, one gets the sense Jesus knew where the world's problems lie. In the final analysis, the problems aren't embedded in our social structures. The problem lies within the human heart, with all its conceits, anger and greed. We are the hearts who create these social structures.

Here John's Gospel account of the feeding of the five thousand tells us a great deal. As the loaves and fish work their way up the hillside, the multitude begins to realize a miracle is taking place. Caught up in the excitement, John writes of the crowd, "They wanted to seize Jesus and make him their king." Jesus was their perfect candidate, the politician who could right all the wrongs and deliver on peace and prosperity; after all he could perform miracles. But the story says Jesus wouldn't have anything to do with human coronations, as John tells us that Jesus turned from the crowd and walked into the wilderness, alone.

It's the next day, when the crowd catches up to Jesus, John begins to tell the story he really wants to tell. They ask him for more of the same bread they ate the day before, but Jesus says so much more is offered. He offers them living bread. Eventually the conversation goes nowhere, with the crowd only wanting to talk about a full stomach while Jesus wants to talk about the fullness of life. Unable to see what is placed before them, what's on the table, this time it's the crowd who turns its back on Jesus, leaving him with only the twelve. The world will always clamor for bread which fills us for the moment. Christians support that kind of bread, but we also see its limitations. Those limitations are our limitations. The world is lost because we are lost. History is filled with grand calls for hope and change, only to return to our broken world because we return to our same old selves. It's only in this offer of living bread, Christ's beckoning call to communion with him, we will find what we're looking for. Only when we take and eat, we will begin to know real justice. Only then will we begin to change the world.

Chapter Nine

Ten Questions Christians Must Answer

James 1:5 If any of you is lacking in wisdom, ask God, who gives to all generously and it will be given unto you. But ask in faith, never doubting, for the one who doubts is like a wave of the sea, driven and tossed by the wind; for the doubter, being double-minded and unstable in every way, must not expect to receive anything from the Lord.

Having lunch with a friend, I couldn't help but overhear a conversation at the next table. Two young men, each with beards and backpacks had that look of itinerants new to the city. I began to listen as one of them posed in rapid fire succession, a series of religious questions to the other. What is the origin of sin? What is our means of salvation? In similar manner the other man fired back with equally quick answers, consisting of one line Bible verses. I admired their zeal and most of their answers made sense, but I had some doubts about their flashcards for Jesus approach. For the world in which we now live, I'm not sure many will be persuaded.

Their conversation gave me pause for another reason. Christians need to be careful in trying to supply simple answers in a complicated world. Job tells us as much when we find him hurling up towards the heavens a series of agonizing questions, "Why am I suffering? Why do the wicked prosper?" The Book of Job then introduces his three friends who gather around in order to console him, but when they begin to offer nice tidy answers for Job's suffering, he isn't consoled. Eventually Job loses patience, dismissing them all. Later when God finally appears on the scene, he too sweeps aside their simple explanations, declaring from the whirlwind, "Who darkens my counsel?"

Only God and Job will have a talk. That's because Job is willing to go beyond the easy answers. The first question posed by God properly reorients Job as well as the reader concerning the deep questions of life, "Where were you when I laid the foundations of the earth? Tell me, if you have understanding. Who determined its measurements - surely you know?" We cannot answer. We don't know the length and breadth of the universe nor how it began. If we don't know such things, why is it we wax so eloquently about the workings of life?

God then takes Job on a breathtaking journey, a soliloquy in which God tells him how the heavenly beings rejoiced at the time of creation, how he made the wild animals unbridled in their freedom. In this freedom God talks about life's struggle even its cruel moments. He tells Job about the ominous Leviathan who resides in the dark and deep waters and God's decision to contend with it, telling us that he enters into this struggle alongside us. When God concludes we're left to wonder, what then is the answer? It's in Job's response we begin to grasp something, "I know that you can do all things. Therefore I have uttered what I did not understand, things too wonderful for me, which I did not know." We realize Job has received something far greater than an answer. He has been given perspective, one expansive and vast. He's also heard the voice of God, which tells us of a God who knows us intimately, and who eventually responds to our prayers. Mystery remains, but we now have a new way of seeing. We've been given all we need to navigate through this difficult life. With this we can say along with Job, we have been given something "too wonderful."

This is the caution I urge upon the reader with the following series of questions and answers. Fifty years ago a grandparent could settle everything by replying "Because the Bible says so," but those days are over and perhaps fortunately so. Christians are now forced to look deeper and think harder about what they believe. With the tables turned and the secular world now asking these questions, often in a spirit of antagonism, we have to answer. Yet if we travel down the road Job has journeyed, we will eventually find what he found. Faith provides us with a deep understanding, a compelling stance towards life, even if they don't always come in the form of answers.

How can you believe in a good and all-powerful God when we live in a world filled with pain and suffering?

Once during a Sunday school class, I responded to this question by asking a question of my own, again hoping for perspective rather than an answer. Holding up a ruler next to the lectern, I said "Here's a magic wand. If you decide to waive it over your children, they will never know suffering or loss. They will never encounter any obstacles in life. Now, who wants to take this magic wand and waive it over them?"

There were no takers, but why? There is nothing we love in this world more than our children, so why would we not exempt them from all the problems and pain we know they'll encounter? Perhaps our reticence is instructive, telling us something we can't quite articulate. Likely the magic wand question causes us to think back upon our own experience. I've noticed that when friends are talking casually, we talk about good times, but whenever a conversation turns more intimate, we often bring up the hard times. Our recollections are painful, even bitter, yet for some reason we don't want to completely erase them. Perhaps we instinctively know something: whatever courage, perseverance or empathy we now possess was a lesson from the most profound of all teachers, suffering. Can we not say that all of our meaningful victories in life are one's hard fought?

In this counter-question we can't say we've found our answer, but we have found our way. There are a few things we do know. God doesn't waive his magic wand and in some recess we know a perfect God must have a perfect reason; one which we cannot yet fathom but one we can still accept. It doesn't lessen the pain, but it allows us to bear it. Somehow in all of this we know there is a God who is deeply involved, and who is fully invested in who we shall become. This we also know, in this often painful process of 'becoming' God didn't exempt himself from our own human suffering. He knows our pain even more intimately than we do. What more do we need to know?

I used to call myself religious, but now I tell people I'm spiritual.

This is a trendy statement on several fronts. By calling yourself spiritual, you're letting people know you're open-minded and tolerant of all beliefs. There is something good in that of course. It also has a pseudo-intellectual appeal, telling people in effect that your inquiry of life's options is one fully ranged. All of this solicits the admiration of the like-minded, but does this ambiguous stance of spiritually really engage the deeper questions of life? Does not the vague term of 'spiritual' reveal a person who has no real commitments, or at the very least someone who isn't pursuing a path towards something we can claim as true? As G.K. Chesterton wrote, "When people stop believing in God they don't believe in nothing, they believe in anything."

True spirituality involves an engagement, an inquiry, a questioning and probing meant to lead us somewhere outside of ourselves. In the case of a true spiritual quest, we look for such things as meaning, purpose and love. How can we invoke the 'great whatever' for such things? Ask the spiritual person to tell you about the object of their worship, and you won't get anything resembling worship. You may get something nebulous such as a life force or the cosmos, but why worship the created instead of the Creator? The spiritual person will counter with "How can you know?" as if theirs is the stronger philosophical stance. But neither side can offer real proofs. Can we stack up enough arguments of this world, spiritual, philosophical or scientific, in order to reach another world? Christians differentiate themselves in several ways. For them, such knowledge doesn't come from within. We believe we know what we think we know from God's reach down, from One who wants to be known and wants to be in relation with us. Such knowledge may be incomplete and mediated, yet still constitutes reliable knowledge. This is the paradox of the man who calls himself spiritual. In his pluralistic stance he is cut off from everything outside himself, while the Christian stance is open. The spiritual person is the Enlightenment man closed off from mystery because his search is confined inward. Only someone who seeks will ever find.

How can Christians be so exclusive by claiming in John 14:6, 'I am the way and the truth and the life. No one comes to the Father except through me.' What about the primitive man who has never heard of Jesus?

The question of this skeptic reveals several underlying assumptions. First, by questioning the means by which God has chosen for salvation, he is in effect substituting his own cultural standards with our plans somehow overriding God's plans. It is also insincere because it casts Christianity in a false light. God, as revealed through Christ, is for the entire world. His commission is universal and his forgiveness from the cross is extended to all. Christianity was the first to proclaim the most radical concept of diversity as found in Paul's letter to the Galatians, "There is neither Jew nor Greek, slave or free, male or female, for you are one in Jesus Christ," a statement beyond revolutionary when it was written to a highly stratified first century world.

With respect to the primitive and isolated man who has never heard of Jesus, let's again ask a counter-question of our skeptic. "When it comes to your own situation, having heard the Gospel, isn't this for you a hypothetical question? Doesn't the Gospel force a person to say yes or no, rather than invoking a theoretical man he doesn't know?" Still, let's entertain our hypothetical man for a moment. In yielding to God sovereignty, Christianity does proclaim Christ as the way towards salvation, but this doesn't necessarily limit the ways in which Christ may work in our world. This is where the Holy Spirit is central to our faith. In the Gospels Christ promises to return in the form of the Holy Spirit, something the Bible symbolically portrays as the wind, invisible, taking paths and shaping the landscape in ways we cannot perceive. Can anyone say Christ, working in this manner, cannot speak to anyone and work his salvation through anyone, without having a formal name attached?

I don't go to Church anymore. Besides, you don't have to go to Church to be a Christian.

Some statements, like this one, are literally true but are in essence falsehoods. They also reveal how much we like to rationalize. If someone said, "You really don't have to eat well and exercise in order to live a long healthy life," technically they're correct. You can live a long life without doing those things, but you'd consider their statement absurd. No, we don't have to go to Church, but why did Jesus ask Peter to be its founder? Why did he commission Paul? Isn't community necessary for communion?

Why don't we just love each other?

While gathering my notes after a Sunday school presentation, a man approached the podium with a question, "My daughter is home from college this weekend. When I asked her to come to Church with me today, she said 'Dad, why don't we just love each other and leave out all the religious stuff?'"

She expresses a nice sentiment. Who can argue with loving each other? But we don't live by sentiments, nor can we stake our lives upon them. Truth is what we seek, searching for something upon which we can stake our lives upon. I'm guessing her critique of organized religion was part of the cultural script supplied on campus, with high-minded ideals of love, peace and harmony substituted in religion's place, free spirits unencumbered by our human flaws. One question gets to the heart of the matter. Can we really love one another, in the truest sense of the word, apart from God? Do we possess the selfless capacity to love fully and freely? An honest answer, and the Christian answer, is that we cannot. History, including our own personal history, is a testament to this conclusion.

In Luke's Gospel a rich young man approaches Jesus with a question, "Good teacher, what must I do to inherit eternal life?" Jesus' answer seems puzzling, "Why do you call me good? No one is good but God alone." It's baffling because he's not only good; he is the Son of God. Likely Jesus' response is intended to challenge the assumption behind the young man's question, the assumption that a teacher can impart to us some moral or ethical lesson which will give us eternal life. Jesus' rejoinder, "Only God is good," is an attempt to reorient the man towards the path his search must take, elevating their discussion to its proper heights. If only God is good, then in our search for what is good, for what is noble and life-giving, we begin with God alone. How can this infinite God, Creator of us and our universe, not be the source of all that is good?

Our sentimental responses often turn out to be nothing more than exercises in avoidance. Touting some ephemeral universal love, something which has never existed in the history of mankind, allows us to remain in charge. We can live by our own standards, with love, duty and morality ours to define and manipulate with our rationalizations. Perhaps this was the calling beyond our own self-fixed boundaries in the Sermon on the Mount, "Be ye perfect as your

Father in heaven is perfect." Being perfect is likely something you'll never hear on campus.

How can Christians say the Bible is the Word of God when it contains inconsistencies and mythical stories?

What you think about the Bible likely depends upon certain suppositions you bring to it before you ever turn the first page. If you're looking for a history book, filled with facts and dates along with social or political commentary, you won't get that for one reason. It was never intended to be that kind of book.

Stepping back, we need to reflect upon the task set before the Biblical writers, especially those of the New Testament. Think of what they saw and what they heard. A man who claims to be God comes into our world. He performs miracles and he lives the most extraordinary life ever lived. He dies and then comes back in the form of a resurrected body. The writers claim all of this to be historical, yet at the same time they understood such facts as transcending history, supplying nothing less than all of human history's meaning and fulfillment. How can such events and such truths be proclaimed? Can we tell this story in the same way we tell other stories? Can we reduce statements such as Apostle Paul's, "In Christ we are a new creation," to our everyday explanations? This is both the burden and perspective of those who were writing the Bible. The Transcendent, inaccessible and beyond, has made a decision to be accessible and to dwell among us. This is one reason why the Gospels have little interest in supplying us with historical markers and social perspective. They don't even bother to tell us what Jesus looked like.

For them the story was too large and the claims made too great. They knew ordinary storytelling and ordinary language were inadequate to the task. Yet only by telling a story and by using symbolic language can we come close. Its truths can only be conveyed by such a vessel, theologically couched to convey a meaning beyond historical facts alone. Still, with all these limitations, the writers were able write beyond their human abilities by way of Christ's promise to his disciples in the Gospel of John just before his death, "The Advocate, the Holy Spirit, whom my Father will send in my name, will teach you everything and remind you of all that I have said to you." The writers are very human, very fallible, yet God finds a way to speak through us. In short it's complicated, and for those who want simple answers, Christian doctrine is not the place to look. Perhaps we should ask one simple question of the Bible. Do you believe this God, who loves us so passionately and wants us to know him intimately, would bequeath to us a guide so unreliable that we would be left in the dark? How you answer this question likely will answer all your other questions about the Bible.

Church history is filled with scandal and disgrace. It's also filled with hypocrites.

Church history is in fact filled with scandal and the Church is in fact filled with hypocrites. All of human history is filled with scandal and the world is full of hypocrites. Those so antagonistic to the Church usually aren't just talking about the Church, they're describing humanity, a world filled with sins we all share. Most often than not, their judgments are without any balance whatsoever. If we judge things by their worst example, nothing of this world will ever survive. The Bible is brutally honest in a way few others religions are. Its heroines and heroes are very flawed people. Prior to Pentecost, the disciples are a bunch of spiritual failures who abandon Jesus at the cross. Paul's letters to his first century Churches reveal deeply dysfunctional communities. King David maneuvers one of his soldiers into certain death so he can take his wife. How's that for honesty?

The question becomes this. What separates the Church as the Body of Christ, filled with flawed humans, apart from our otherwise shared human condition outside the Church? Christians shouldn't hold themselves out as privileged, whether it's concerning sin or salvation. We see ourselves as fallen and salvation as extended to all. But when it comes to truth, Christians don't say 'my truth,' rather they claim a truth received, one we're still trying to work out in our lives, often with great difficulty. Whenever the Church or Christians lose sight of their dependence upon God, they have fallen short. Whenever they are reoriented to this stance, the Church and Christianity have flourished. So, perhaps the real question is one that should be redirected back to the skeptic. What is the way to which you can point as your own way towards truth and grace?

With so many other religions in the world, how can Christianity claim its faith is the one which is absolutely true?

For one thing, the Judeo-Christian claims are in fact unique. Its truths don't depend upon some inner search for wisdom. It's based upon the claim of the Jews that God intervened in their history and spoke to them as a people. It's based upon disciples who claim Jesus Christ walked the earth, teaching, healing and revealing who God is. Nothing of its essence is subjective. Again and again the claim is simply 'this happened.' Other religious claims may compete, but competition doesn't necessarily mean subtraction. One must deal with the Jewish and Christian claims in terms of true or false, yes or no, because that's how they're presented to us.

With respect to the question concerning the plurality of religions, a counter-question should again bring matters into clearer focus. Ask them, "Do you believe all men and women are created equal?" Likely you'll get a yes, but not all people consider this assertion of equality to be true. There is a plurality of opinions ranging from the caste system to cultures which relegate women to inferior roles. Does this diversity of opinion suddenly render untrue their prior truth claim regarding equality?

Why Are Christians So Judgmental?

They're not supposed to be, especially when Jesus says, "Do not judge so you will not be judged." On my way to a meeting in downtown Nashville, I passed through our entertainment district, making my way through the crowded sidewalks filled with tourists and country music booming from the dozens of bars and honkey-tonks. Jostling amid the tourists, I suddenly heard a voice rising slightly above the din. Drawing closer, I saw a young man no more than twenty years old, standing on a small wooden box. Bible in hand, he was doing some old time street preaching. I was expecting an angry rant against rowdy music and drinking, but as I slowed my walk, it sounded like a thoughtful message. From his tone, he wasn't calling out the crowd, he was calling them in.

Most of the tourists passed by without glancing in his direction. He wasn't the attraction they came to see. As I approached, I gave him a quick thumbs up, as if to say 'keep preaching.' He nodded in my direction, giving me a 'God bless you,' picking up where he had left off. Just then one tourist, regaled in his camouflage shorts, fanny pack and cowboy hat, turned in his direction shouting, "You're judging me!" With a wry smile the street preacher calmly replied, "I think you just judged me."

Their brief exchange, I believe, reflects a modern day confusion about judgment. Likely it also exposes a cultural evasion as well. From what I could tell, our preacher wasn't condemning anyone atop his wooden box. He was simply declaring something as true and real as the force of gravity, God does judge. As to why, how and when, Christians should resist peering into their neighbor's souls as only God can do. But the tourist seemed to be chafing against any notion of judgment, likely read from the modern script of free expression and individual lifestyle choices. We can retreat into these seemingly open-minded expressions, but are they a refuge from the reality that God does judge?

Perhaps the greater confusion arises from our inability to see that God's judgment and God's love are one in the same. He isn't petulant and angry at us one moment, then changing his mind and suddenly compassionate. If your child has an addiction, you wouldn't respond with a nonjudgmental hug. Instead you would summon a righteous anger against the addiction, a severe response because you know it will rob your child of their full potential. You can see the despair and darkness awaiting them. In some way this may give us a glimpse of God's judgment. He sees each of us in our full and glorious potential. He dreams a far greater dream over us than we ever could. Anything short of that, God will wrest from us our idols and our addictions. That's what God's love does.

Why do Christians think they need a reward for doing something good?

Before we begin examining the motives of Christians, let's look at everyone's motivation, believers and nonbelievers. We all want to be noticed. We all subtly telegraph our good deeds. Unfortunately the esteem of others is important to us.

There is, of course, the promise of eternal life to believers, but the majority of the Biblical narrative doesn't talk about that. For the most part, Christianity makes demands upon how we live in the here and now, without strictly tied to an afterlife. The Christian life in this world has its own rewards. When Jesus says to his disciples, "My peace I give to you," he gives his promise in the present, not some far off world to come. Still, when we consider rewards, Christians aren't supposed to think of them in the same manner as the rest of the world. Besides, the call to take up one's cross is hardly something our culture would call a reward.

Once again, a question may get to the heart of the matter, asking of the scoffer or nonbeliever, "Do you love your parents only so you'll receive your inheritance?" If so their relationship is purely transactional, whereas the Christian faith is purely relational. Ultimately we follow a Person as the object of our worship. The Biblical means of describing this comes in the way of analogies such as Father and children, friends, brothers and sisters, all relational. We strive not so much towards a distant future in heaven; rather we are motivated to love because we have already been deeply loved. Gratitude is our foundation.

Chapter Ten

The Public Square

1 Corinthians 2:4 My speech and my proclamation were not with plausible words of wisdom, but with a demonstration of the Spirit and of power, so that your faith may not rest on human wisdom but on the power of God.

Before we can begin talking about a Christian response to the revolution, first we need to reclaim some historical perspective on what I call the public square. By that term I mean the democratic competition of ideas and beliefs, whether in the mainstream media, politics or any other civic engagement. The public square was once a unique American strength, an edifying voice where we gave expression to shared moral responsibilities, defining and refining how we should best live together. That public square no longer exists. Gone are the rational debates necessary for a cohesive society. Gone is civility, with everything now seen through the prism of rights claimed by aggrieved parties vying for power rather than truth. Once seized, the conversation becomes a platform for silencing rivals. No longer is there language directed towards the common good. The loss of religious speech in the public square isn't just a loss for Christianity but a loss for freedom itself.

As the moral voice has receded, what were once shared questions are individualized or reduced to sentimental platitudes, with civic conversations now lacking in depth and content. This erosion has been accomplished by two artful deceptions. One voices shouts 'separation of Church and state,' as if it were an inviolate Constitutional principle. It is not, nor has it ever been. It is only a phrase lifted from a letter of Thomas Jefferson addressed to the Baptist Association of Danbury, Connecticut in 1802. The Constitution says only this about the relationship of government and religion: "Congress shall make no law respecting the establishment of religion or prohibiting the free exercise thereof." The initial phrase is referred to as the establishment clause, the second is called the free exercise clause.

James Madison, its initial drafter, had something specific in mind when he conceived of the establishment clause. In his time Virginia had designated the Church of England as the official religion of the Commonwealth, even levying taxes on its citizens for its support. The strongest advocacy for the inclusion of the establishment clause came from other denominations, wanting to ensure that the federal government would not do the same. Diversity of faith, not the diminution of faith, was its original intent. The intent of the free exercise clause however was far more expansive. It was adopted upon the principle that the government should refrain from interfering in all religious expressions or affairs, both public and private.

This balance of one narrow legal concept and the other expansive, held for almost two hundred years until the U.S. Supreme Court, caught up in the spirit of the 1960s, suddenly broke with precedent. The majority of justices well knew the traditional strength of the free exercise clause. Only shrewd legal maneuvering and the invention of a new legal premise, one never conceived of by the Constitution's framers, could weaken it. They elevated one part of the Constitution from its original context to bring down another, turning the establishment clause against free exercise. Suddenly something as simple as a prayer on public property or on a football field was a form of establishment, defying not only precedent but the clear sense of the word itself. Still, sensing the weakness of its legal reasoning, the Court needed to invent the concept of 'endorsement' as the equivalent of establishment. Words had to be twisted and concepts made vague in order to open a door which was never meant to be opened. Had these justices taken a quick glance at the east portico of their own Supreme Court building, they would have seen the large frieze of Moses holding the Ten Commandments. How a prayer or a traditional religious symbol on federal property constitutes the establishment of any one denomination or the imposition of any particular faith upon an individual, the Court could never say.

The other deception shouts into the square 'neutrality,' a secular claim that the public arena should be some sort of clean slate, thus devoid of faith. But the public square has never been neutral, nor was it ever intended to be. The Constitution envisioned a vigorous competition, with religion having its own say among others. The claim of neutrality is simply a strategy, an attempt to marginalize expressions of faith while secularism can openly promote its own belief system. In another fiction secularism likes to raise the specter of a Christian nation, yet it's unable to point to any period in our history where beliefs have been imposed. The rise of agnosticism in our country should be ample evidence that orthodox Christianity, at its core, is apolitical. All the Church wants is a place to stand and speak alongside all others. It doesn't need a privileged space because it knows it possesses a unique voice and message, one empowered by the Holy Spirit, the only voice and the only message capable of touching the deepest cord in the human heart. It needs no office, no government and no control of the forum, just a place to speak the Word.

Rebels Without a Cause and Without a Compass

When did this irreligious voice elbow its way into the square, shouting down our history of faith in the marketplace which once spoke of virtues and character? When did we stop talking about a shared morality?

In a previous chapter we observed the choice made by Europe as it found itself lying in the rubble of World War II. By refusing to look into the mirror and confront its dark side, something Enlightenment thinking couldn't come to grips with, Europe adopted yet another human-centric philosophy in the form of postmodernism. Postwar America found itself in a very different place. Rather than the wreckage of war, we were lying in a bed of roses. The conflict had only touched our shores lightly. Instead of the economic struggles of a war-torn Europe, World War II had lifted America out of the remnants of the depression, awakening an economic colossus.

Those who lived through the depression, who had won the war and returned home to build a dynamic new country, were rightfully given the name of our Greatest Generation. All they had previously known was sacrifice, so as they came home in 1945, the national mood changed dramatically. It was finally time to kick back and enjoy life, and with a new economy lifting the middle class as never before, it was also time for new houses and new cars. Upbeat music and television reflected the good times, the mood was light and this Greatest Generation deserved it.

There was one problem with this live a little mindset. It walked straight through the doors of America's churches. Gone was the Old Testament view of life as a never ending struggle, requiring constant vigilance and self-denial. This generation had already picked up their cross, and they were tired of carrying it. The times were eventually reflected by the title of a popular sixties book, "I'm OK, You're OK." In this relaxed atmosphere, pop psychology easily mixed with traditional faith. Religion had become therapeutic, lessening its demands, no longer posing to us the hard questions or asking us to bear burdens. In a society gravitating towards consumption and excess, we simply affirmed ourselves. We were OK.

Along with the new cars and the new houses came the Baby Boomers, children born between 1946 and 1964. They were the real beneficiaries of this live it up culture. Parenting was far more relaxed. The depression era advice to steel one's self because life is hard, gave way to new counsel of blazing your own path. The Greatest Generation also made an unspoken vow over their children. They would never have to experience what they had gone through. They would give their children all the things they never had.

One gift would go missing however, the gift of traditional faith. Families still went to Church, in fact they went in record numbers during the 1960s, but the Biblical worldview with its suspicion of the world's ways, of restraint in behavior and humility as our greatest virtue, were no longer at our core. The family Bible, passed down for generations, was now somewhere in the attic. If we want to know why the traditions of faith mean so little to Millennials, we only have to look to their parents. They never took it all that seriously.

One of those gifts to the Baby Boomers was college, as they enrolled in record numbers. Living in the land of plenty, surrounded by the carefree atmosphere of college, the cultural revolution of the 1960s and 1970s now seems inevitable. The spoiled child will bite the feeding hand. The Baby Boomers lacked an external challenge, something every generation needs in order to define itself. With no mountains to climb, they took a narcissistic turn inward. It was all about them and everything in their way had to be brought down. It was anti-establishment, anti-military, anti-tradition and anti-capitalism, rejecting everything which protected them, raised them and coddled them. They were like the barbarians overturning the tables, not sure why, just their primal self-assertion. They lived by trite slogans such as 'tune in, turn on and drop out,' seizing power simply because they could, and they wanted it now because no one ever told them they had to wait.

Adrift from traditions which were never passed down, along with the off to college parting words of simply finding yourself, their aimless road was personified by the self-indulgent psychedelic school bus ride across the country. It had no destination, just the immersion in sex, drugs and rock n roll. Even religion was a cafeteria of personal choice, whether the deeper consciousness of an LSD trip or the Far East guru of the moment handing out tired expressions.

The students were able to seize the moment because they were surrounded by enablers, by parents who sent them off without structures of convention, by a self-therapy Church which had lost its voice in psycho-babble, leaving our minds unprepared for challenge, along with a university system abdicating its traditional responsibility of molding young people into responsible citizens. The Sixties counterculture was unable to articulate any coherent philosophy, but without its knowledge, it was living one. They were disciples of Descartes, eschewing tradition and seeking knowledge only from their inner selves. They were Kantians who defined their own reality and decided their own natural laws. They were the new Hegelians, declaring their own utopia of peace and love.

In looking back we tend to frame all of this within the Viet Nam War, but that's too simple to explain their acting out, the drug culture, religion de jure and their opposition to just about everything. Few of the protesters or their leaders ever set foot in Southeast Asia. Other wars, such as Korea, were also unpopular. Viet Nam was only a convenient launching point for a self-absorbed ideology with no goal or philosophical roots to call upon. The protesters sensed the war was their elders' weak spot, an Achilles heel poorly conceived and carried out, so it became a point of exploitation. Like so many other self-righteous causes without a real cause, it stood only upon the perceived sins of others.

Eventually the multicolored bus ride ran out of gas. The hippies graduated and soon found the system they once condemned to be very useful in making money. Weak dogma soon cedes to comfort. Although their flower power ideology eventually lost its edge as it receded into the national background, ideas have a way of living on. The damage to the public square was irreparable. No longer rooted in American tradition, it became a shouting match without depth or moral content. Henceforth the public square would be dominated by the naked assertion of rights. We began to look to the law and to politics to perform tasks once accomplished by faith and tradition.

This fundamental shift in national speech, from the moral to the purely political, would have astonished early Americans. In their search to find the most basic foundation for our democratic rights, the signers of the Declaration of Independence didn't draw from the Enlightenment or any other philosophical construct. They looked to religion: "We find these truths to be self-evident, that all men are created equal, that they are endowed by their Creator with certain inalienable rights, that among those are life, liberty and the pursuit of happiness." This is the forgotten ground of our national identity as well as the ground of our freedoms, our Creator.

The History of the Public Square

We're so distanced emotionally and intellectually from the original spirit of the American public square, it's hard to remember anything else. But we can reach back to rediscover something of its essence. That's what Alexis de Tocqueville (1805-1856) was seeking in his travels across America. A French diplomat and political scientist, his two volume work 'Democracy in America,' still stands as perhaps the most insightful analysis of early American culture.

De Tocqueville was searching for the source of what he saw as a unique American dynamism. In time he believed he located it, in something he called the political consequences of religion. "Upon my arrival in the United States, the religious aspect of the country was the first thing that struck my attention; and the longer I stayed, the more I perceived the great political consequences resulting from this new state of things. In France I had always seen the spirit of religion and the spirit of freedom marching in opposite directions but in America I found they were intimately united."

Religious speech should be of great interest to everyone, not just to believers but for the sake of freedom itself. Whenever one freedom is taken away, all our other freedoms are placed in jeopardy. Reflecting the spirit of our Declaration of Independence, de Tocqueville found religion not to be just one beneficial influence among others, but something fundamental to the public square. In faith he saw American's underlying strength, its means of preserving the spirit of democracy from becoming a mobocracy. Law and government he understood, were far easier to manipulate for our personal benefit than faith. This same idea stood behind the various checks and balances built into our original government. The court system was removed from voters. The Senate was initially elected by state legislatures rather than the public. Amending the Constitution was meant to be a difficult and exhaustive process.

De Tocqueville gave voice to this early American spirit, perhaps in a way only an outside observer could articulate, "I sought for the keys to the greatness and genius of America in her harbors, in her fertile fields and boundless forests and world of commerce... in her institutions of learning. I sought for it in her democratic Congress and her matchless Constitution. Not until I went into the churches of America and heard her pulpit flow with righteousness did I understand the secret of her genius and power."

This critical role of religion in our nation's life was expressed earlier by our first citizen, George Washington. Stepping down after his second term as President, Washington wanted to give his country one last gift in the form of advice. He saw democracy as a fragile thing, wondering if it would survive all the challenges he saw ahead. Washington had led us into battle, he secured for us a stable government, and now he wanted the words of his Farewell Address of 1796 to lead us into a distant future, "But a solicitude for your welfare, which cannot end with my life and apprehension of your dangers, urge me to offer you solemn contemplation which appears to be all-important to your permanency of your felicity as a people."

Washington would have found today's shrill public speech loathsome. The Founding Fathers envisioned a far different square, one driven by sound and rational argument rather than raw emotions of competing interest groups. They would have found it irrational for matters of truth to be established solely by political contest. His Farewell Address included a long list of potential dangers awaiting a nascent country, warning us against the formation of political parties, against foreign entanglements as well as "designing men who would exploit and excite sectional differences." We've since suffered from ignoring Washington's advice. Political parties have fractured our country. Foreign entanglements have led us into unnecessary wars. Prophetically he foresaw these 'designing men' who would plunge us into a Civil War. Washington had something else to say about democracy, something he called its 'indispensable support.' He knew democracy wasn't self-sustaining. In order for it to survive, it needed an underlying morality, one which could only come from religion.

> Of all the dispositions and habits which lead to political prosperity, religion and morality are indispensable supports. In vain would that man claim the tribute of patriotism, who should labor to subvert these great pillars of human happiness, these firmest props of the duties of men and citizens. The mere politician, equally with the pious man, ought to respect and to cherish them. A volume could not trace all their connections with private and public felicity. Let it simply be asked: Where is the security for property, for reputation, for life if the sense of religious obligation deserts the oaths which are instruments of investigation in courts of justice? And let us with caution indulge the supposition that morality can be maintained without religion. Whatever may be conceded to the influence of refined education on minds of peculiar structure, reason and experience both forbid us to expect that national morality can prevail in exclusion of religious principle.

Not quite a hundred years later, another President would share with the country his own personal reflections concerning the role of faith in American life, Abraham Lincoln. This time it was needed for healing, to put a nation back together, as Lincoln searched for unifying and restorative words in his Second Inaugural Address. Along with the Gettysburg Address, it is considered his finest speech, both engraved upon the walls of the Lincoln Memorial. But before we read a portion of his Second Inaugural, we need to reflect upon what Lincoln and the country had endured, asking what may have been Lincoln's thoughts as he took pen in hand.

Four years earlier he stood on a railroad platform in Springfield, Illinois saying goodbye to his hometown, one he would never see again. At the time Lincoln faced a crisis greater than any other President-elect. The South was already taking steps to secede, seizing federal armories and assets. Within a few months of taking office, the first shots of the Civil War were fired at Fort Sumter. Soon the hopes of the North for a quick and easy war were dashed by defeat after defeat. With a distinct American ingenuity on display in the realm of warfare, new tactics born of railroads, telegraph and even ironclad submarines, a carnage ensued that was far beyond anything the country expected, as more soldiers died in the Civil War than all other American wars combined.

As the war dragged on, popular support for Lincoln vanished. Criticism of his leadership by both the press and Congress was withering. It appeared that Lincoln, who held a deep reverence for the Founding Fathers and the Constitution since childhood, would become the President who would preside over its dissolution. Personal tragedy then followed when his youngest son Willie died at age eleven in the White House. Soon thereafter Lincoln's lifelong battle with deep depression returned.

It was likely during this period that Lincoln pulled from his desk a sheet of paper and wrote across the top, 'Meditation Upon the Divine Will.' Discovered only after his death by his personal secretary Nicholas Hay, it was never meant to be read by anyone else. It was a personal note, addressed only to God.

> The Will of God prevails. In great contests each party claims to act in accordance with the will of God. Both may be, and one must be, wrong. God cannot be for and against the same thing at the same time. In the present civil war it is quite possible that God's purpose is something different from the purpose of either party, and yet the human instrumentalities, working just as they do, are the best adaptation to affect His purpose. I am almost ready to say that this

is probably true, that God wills this contest, and wills that it shall not end yet. By his mere great power, on the minds of the now contestants, He could have either saved or destroyed the Union without a human contest. Yet the contest began and, having begun He could give the final victory to either side any day. Yet the contest proceeds.

Lincoln's search, to discern the will of God during the darkest of times, was later given its full expression in his Second Inaugural Address of 1865. In that year the war was coming to a close, all but won. Lincoln was returned to office when only a few months earlier his reelection appeared impossible. His depression finally lifted. The Union he cherished so deeply, once calling it the "last best hope of the earth," would soon to be restored. Sitting down to compose what would be his final speech, Lincoln surely had one overarching thought. This God had heard his prayers and this God was faithful.

For this occasion he wouldn't give a political speech. The country needed to heal a deep wound, not reopen it. There would be no triumphant declaration of victory. Too many had died for that. Lincoln had something to say rising far above politics. He would share with the country his hard fought faith, imparting to us wisdom learned on his knees. Lincoln now saw the nation and the war in far grander terms, seeing it as part of a far larger human drama held firmly in the hands of God. Like the Old Testament prophet who spoke a hard truth to Israel, of its sin, of judgment and of a distant hope, Lincoln would talk about our own sin of slavery, a war of judgment and finally of our redemption. After a few brief introductory remarks, he turns to this deeper message he wants to share. Unlike any Presidential speech before or after, Lincoln in essence delivers a sermon.

> Neither party expected for the war the magnitude or the duration which it has already attained. Each looked for an easier triumph and a result less fundamental and astounding. Both read the same

> Bible and prayed to the same God, and each invoked His aid against the other. It may seem strange that any men should dare to ask a just God's assistance in wringing their bread from the sweat of other men's faces, but let us judge not, that we be not judged. The prayers of both could not be answered. That of neither has been answered fully. The Almighty has His own purposes. Woe unto the world because of offenses; for it need be that offenses come, but woe to that man by whom the offense cometh.

Before one can begin the process of healing, there must be a time of repentance. The way forward can only be traveled when we've turned from the wrong path taken. Newspaper accounts of the inauguration described the palpable anger of the North with placards in the crowd saying 'No mercy to the rebels.' They came to hear Lincoln declare victory and to take the South to task, but that isn't what they got. Instead Lincoln shows great balance, declaring that neither party wanted war and both prayed to the same God. With incredible restraint he refuses to invoke judgment upon the South and asks his audience to do the same. With the phrase, "The Almighty has His own purposes," Lincoln then lifts his speech to the theological ground he wants a nation to hear. He will share with us what he has learned in the darkness and what he has now seen in the light of day.

> "If we shall suppose that American slavery is one of those offenses which, in the providence of God, needs to come, but which, having continued through His appointed time, He now wills to remove, and that He gives to both North and South this terrible war as the woe to those by whom the offense came, shall we discern therein any departure from those divine attributes which the believers in a living God always ascribe to Him?"

Lincoln as the prophet lays before the country its sin of slavery. He lays before it the judgment of God, the woes of this terrible war. You would have expected him to say the South gave us this war, but Lincoln now sees the war through God's eyes. Surprising, likely shocking to his listeners, he doesn't say the South gave them this war. He says God gave this war of judgment to both sides. The sins of the South were there for all to see with its slave traders and plantation owners, but what of the North? Its hands were also bloodied by profit, its banks financed the crops, its mills turned the cotton into garments. The declaration of our Founding Fathers eighty-nine years earlier, that all men are created equal, meant the country had long been living a lie. God in his righteousness would now remove a nation's sin.

> Fondly do we hope, fervently do we pray, that this mighty scourge of war may speedily pass away. Yet, if God wills that it continue until all the wealth piled by the bondsman's two hundred and fifty years of unrequired toil shall be sunk, and until every drop of blood drawn with the lash shall be paid by another drawn with the sword, as we said three thousand years ago, so still it must be said 'the judgments of the Lord are true and righteous altogether.' With malice toward none, with charity for all, with firmness in the right as God has given us to see the right, let us strive on to finish the work we are in, to bind up the nation's wounds, to care for him who shall have borne the battle and for his widow and his orphan, to do all which may achieve and cherish a just and lasting peace among ourselves and with all nations.

Suffering serves no redemptive purpose unless there is some hope at the end of our suffering. The prophets of Israel exposed its sinfulness. They foretold its exile, but they always spoke of a far off hope, of returning home. The prophet told Israel that although they had broken their covenant with God, God would not break his covenant with them. I believe Lincoln, whose knowledge of the Bible was extensive, was compelled to give nothing other than a sermon. God had spoken to his prophet, and he needed to tell the nation what he had heard.

During his address Lincoln quotes from Scripture on five different occasions. Perhaps he knew a country's deep wound could only be healed with a Biblical word, one which he knew would resonate, finding a common ear in both the North and the South. Perhaps he knew a sermon was the only way to bind up a nation's wounds and show us the way forward. Lincoln needed to remind us of something we had forgotten in both slavery and in war. We were still God's people.

It's easy to read these words and resign them to the past, an artifact of words which can no longer be spoken. Yet Lincoln's words are timeless. He speaks what he believes to be an enduring truth. Either God will be invoked for our protection and for our future or he will not. If we say this speech can't be given today, we then have to ask, why not? Another question follows. In our next crisis where will we turn? Who will summon for us words of repentance and hope? Lincoln's words not only tell us about a people who once saw themselves as living under the care and concern of a faithful God, they also tell us how much we have lost.

Chapter Eleven

A Christian Response

John 1:11 He came to what was his own, and his own people did not accept him. But to all who received him, who believed in his name, he gave power to become children of God, who were born, not of blood or of the will of the flesh or the will of man, but of God.

Now we turn to the question asked earlier in Chapter One. In the face of this Post-Christian revolution, what do we do? I'm hopeful that the reader, with a better understanding of how the revolution began, its belief system and its ways of persuasion, will be better prepared to answer this question. It's also my hope that the previous chapters have revealed to you the revolution's inherent weaknesses, its inability to address the most basic of human questions. Seeing how poorly constructed is their Tower of Babel, and how limited is its reach, Christians can begin to reclaim their confidence.

In asking the question of what we should do, we must exercise some caution however. The temptation is to strike out into the world armed with our enthusiasm, attempting to slay all the cultural dragons. This risks getting out in front of Christ rather than heeding his words to follow. Our dragon-slaying impulse may not be the way of the cross. Our call to Christian discipleship is unlike any other calling. It is not a movement which stands alongside other worldly movements. Christians may at times find themselves engaged in politics, since it can be a means of speaking the truth, but an immersion in the political arena or any other secular agenda for that matter, risks confusing such things with the kingdom of God.

This means the question posed to Christians, of what we should do, is by necessity different from all other activist questions. These opening verses from John's Gospel tell us that something must first occur. Prior to taking action, we must become, allowing this Word to transform our lives. Such a summons resists all programmatic approaches. As much as we want a motivational seminar or self-help book showing us the way with ten easy steps to success with Jesus, intuitively we know this isn't the path to be taken.

Throughout his Gospel, John gives shape to this question of becoming. In the first of his seven miracle stories, he presents a wedding at Cana. At first glance Jesus' miracle seems a bit superfluous. Turning water into wine doesn't help anyone. It doesn't cast out any demons. It just keeps the party going. But John places it first because it is foremost, with all other miracles secondary to this one of change, our transformation into children of God. With the setting of a wedding ceremony, we're also told something about the means of our becoming. It begins with a relationship, the joining of two in a lifelong journey, us and Christ.

John gives further shape to this theme in his story of Nicodemus, who comes to Jesus alone at night. Nicodemus is curious, wanting to know more, but he comes with a diminished imagination, referring to Jesus as a rabbi or teacher, then asking about the signs he has performed. Jesus doesn't bother with the premise Nicodemus brings to their encounter. Instead he takes their conversation to heights Nicodemus cannot yet grasp. Far beyond Jesus' teaching and healings, Jesus says there is something primary, we must first be born again.

Still, we have a little of Nicodemus in us all, so we're left wondering in our own small imaginations, how then do we become? At the very least we need some direction, something which points the way. Our questions may be answered in part when we consider the manner in which Jesus called each of his disciples, and how he calls us as well. As he walked by he simply said, "Follow me," offering no explanations as to where they would be going or exactly what they would be doing. For those two words they dropped their nets and walked away from the tax-gathering table. All Jesus added on occasion was the enigmatic statement that they would be fishers of men, something they didn't understand at the time. The invitation to simply follow tells us that this way of becoming isn't an invitation to embrace any principle, philosophy or even some grand human truth. Unlike other faiths, the essence of Christianity and Judaism is wholly relational, as two walk together. Early Christians often referred to their faith as 'the way.' Just like the first disciples, our own call is also a mystery, a way that will be filled with twists and turns, disappointments and triumphs, not exactly knowing what is around the corner. Yet like the first disciples there was one sure thing, Christ was with them every moment. By walking with him for three years, that is how they would eventually become someone new, and that is how they in time would know what to do.

In his closing chapters, called the Farewell Discourse, John tells us how we can undertake this journey when Jesus is physically absent, or for that matter when he sometimes seems spiritually absent. John reminds us that he is very present. As Jesus gathers his disciples around the table for the last time, he knows he must equip them for a journey to continue after his death. He tells them he is leaving, but he tells them he is coming back, and he says his departure is "to their advantage," since this new presence will have a new power, one which is no longer limited by his physical body. Using the metaphor of the vine and the branches, he promises to return in the form of the Holy Spirit, encouraging them, reminding them of his words and teaching them. It doesn't mean the way forward won't be difficult and without obstacles, but it does mean they will overcome all things because, "I will not leave you as orphans."

There's still a Nicodemus in us who wants something more concrete, better directions. More than a few have expressed to me their frustration that sometimes God seems so silent. I've had those same feelings myself. My first thought is to ask how much time they are spending with God, asking whether God can speak through the din and fog of a life filled with busyness and other priorities? Are we not somewhat like the daughter or son who laments they aren't closer to their parents, yet never spending time with them?

The world's noise is our first barrier to overcome in this mysterious way of becoming. In Paradise Lost, John Milton refers to hell as Pandemonium. In C.S. Lewis' Screwtape Letters, the devil's minion charged with corrupting his human says, "Music and silence, how I detest them both." Even without our constant streaming of information and entertainment, Jesus had his own noise to deal with. Everywhere he went there were large crowds shouting for his attention, jostling to get just a glimpse or a touch. Yet with all those urgent needs, the Gospels often tell us that Jesus turned away from the crowd, withdrawing into the wilderness to be alone with his Father. Likely he left behind a few who needed healing, but he could see the far bigger picture of his ministry in the silence of prayer. Alone with his Father he knew the source of his power to heal the world. Alone with his Father he was able to see the path to be taken. He would be given a vision of this kingdom to come. For us it is no different.

In addition to a life of prayer, this call to follow and to become, invites us into the Church. I know this invitation runs counter to today's individualized spirituality, but that's precisely a good reason we should be a part of the Church. Neither character formation nor spiritual formation can be done on our own. We've also forgotten something amid all the epithets and denunciations thrown at the Church by modernity. It is still God's chosen instrument to reconcile the world to himself. With all its sins, upheavals and shortcomings, it remains the Body of Christ. This is of course a mystery, but in part I think it means that in the long run the mission and future of the Church isn't so dependent upon us and our faithfulness, but upon the faithfulness of God. He will chastise the Church, at times he will judge it harshly and he will constantly reform it, but he will never abandon it, telling Peter "The Gates of Hell will never overcome it."

During one of my Interfaith meetings a consensus emerged that the Church would soon modernize and get with the times, morphing into something new. That something new sounded like an outreach charity indistinguishable from any other. They were fine with the Church building houses or digging wells in third world countries, but they seemed embarrassed by associating those good works with the call to Christ. I asked a question of this new Church without Christ, "What happened to Jesus' great commission to make disciples of all nations in the name of the Father, Son and Holy Spirit?" One of them appeared to speak for the majority, "Well, that was back then, but not today." I didn't follow up by asking the exact expiration date of Jesus' words, but I smiled at the thought of this secular snapshot of history. Over the last three thousand years nations have risen and fallen, names of great kings have been forgotten for all time. Languages have vanished from the earth. Yet the Synagogue and the Church are the lone survivors.

Finding the right Church is difficult. If you walk into a place which has little regard for Scripture and tradition, likely it isn't the Body of Christ who would preserve such things for successive generations. If the pulpit sounds more like politics, the refrain of man as the savior of man, it's not the Body of Christ. Everyone is invited into the Church, but we're asked to drop our worldly baggage when we walk through those doors. The Church isn't supposed to be a mirror of the world but a refuge from it. We're invited to come as you are, but not to stay as you are. Haltingly the Church limps along through the ages, yet somehow remains a means of becoming. The other Church to avoid is the congregation with an over-dependence upon emotional appeals. We're supposed to love God with not only our heart and soul, but also our minds. When I read the Gospels, the Jesus I see in my mind's eye doesn't resemble many of today's televangelists. I see him speaking in powerful yet measure tones. I hear him making absolute demands upon us which require more than our feelings, foremost an appeal to our wills.

With the Christian Church under siege, we're left to wonder whether there isn't some sort of blueprint which can serve as a guide, bringing us back to where we were. First we need to remember that the secular verdict of a declining Church is a Western-centric view, with Christianity exploding in Asia and Africa, counting more believers than ever. But we've forgotten something; there is in fact a blueprint we can call upon. It can be found in Paul's letters to the early Church, one he navigated through an unbelieving pagan culture and a hostile government. In a sense things aren't all that different today. Our guide is Pauls' insistence upon Christ alone as the center. It is also found in his fierce insistence that the Gospel be preserved as the Word of God against a constant onslaught of cultural compromises. That wasn't only a formula for the Church's survival. It was a formula for its explosion. Individual Christians can also draw some guidance from the first century. As Rome successively conquered nations, each culture was allowed to continue worshipping its old gods, as long as they agreed to add the Roman gods to the mix. For centuries this synchronism worked for all peoples and beliefs across the Mediterranean, until Rome met up with Judaism and Christianity. Unlike all other religions, they would worship only one God. A similar dynamic presents itself to believers today. Modernity will tolerate a bland form of Christianity. At times it will even extol some of its virtues. But when taken seriously, forsaking all the world's idols and powers for Christ alone, our world will take notice and then lash out.

When you find a Church, likely you'll find it filled with difficult people, folks who pray piously on Sundays and act very differently on Mondays. This is your Church. This is where you should roll up your sleeves and get busy. This is part of God's puzzling yet wonderful choice, enlisting flawed people like us to bring about his kingdom. Why he chooses this chaotic and messy way of saving his world, may tell us something about this journey of becoming. He sees us not only as we are, rather he sees us in the full potential of who we shall one day become. In reading his epistles we see how the Apostle Paul understood this as well. He describes congregations with egos, bickering and bad behavior, but those were the same people he also addressed as 'saints.' Paul too saw us as becoming.

Salt and Light

Matthew 5:13 You are the salt of the earth…..You are the light of the world.

The opening verses of Matthew's Sermon on the Mount describes two groups, "When Jesus saw the crowds, he went up to the mountain and after he sat down, his disciples came to him." One group has made a decision to follow. They ascend, drawing near so they can learn of this impending kingdom of God, while the crowd keeps its distance. Presumably they can overhear Jesus, with the hope that his words will serve as an invitation to break out of the crowd and join the inner circle. Jesus tells his disciples they can begin living in the kingdom right now. "Blessed are those who are poor in spirit, theirs is the Kingdom of Heaven." They no longer live by the rules of the world; no longer do we demand an eye for an eye and a tooth for a tooth. They are no longer citizens of a world gone mad. It has no hold over them. If it strikes out at them they don't strike back.

But Jesus' words serve as much more than a to-do list. He tells them they are the salt of the earth and the light of the world. Here he touches upon our becoming, the new person from which our actions will naturally proceed. The metaphors of salt and light are something of our interior. We are made mostly of saltwater. Salt is a preservative. It works invisibly by taking what is bland and tasteless, bringing out its natural richness. The inner circle is literally called to bring out the world's hidden goodness and to give it life. Our light also comes from within, yet it visibly emanates outward, leading the world out of its darkness.

Jesus' sermon dispels a subtle temptation for new disciples, the temptation that we need to do something big and grand, at least in the world's way of seeing things. He talks about small things which are great in the eyes of God. If we are asked to go a mile, we go two. We mourn and we show mercy. We thirst for righteousness. These may be things only God will ever notice. The temptation is to seek the applause of the world rather than living to hear the words, "Well done my good and faithful servant." If we are faithful in small things, the parable of the talents says we will one day be put in charge of great things.

For most of us our ministry isn't something 'out there.' It's usually right next to us, in our marriages and how we shape our children's lives. It's a light that shines on our neighbor, our local community and at the office. God doesn't engage in skywriting, instead he chooses to work from the particular to the universal. He begins by speaking to one couple, Abraham and Sarah who give birth to a small and seemingly insignificant nation, yet one meant to save the world. Jesus, who likely never walked more than fifty miles from his birthplace, chooses only twelve to travel with him. But these are the concentric circles working outward as the Word is cast into the waters. From the twelve there were hundreds, then thousands, then millions and finally billions.

Compassion

Matthew 9:35 Then Jesus went about all the cities and villages, teaching in their synagogue, and proclaiming the good news of the kingdom, and curing every disease and every sickness. When he saw the crowds, he had compassion for them because they were harassed and helpless, like sheep without a shepherd. Then he said to his disciples, 'the harvest is plentiful, but the laborers are few; therefore ask the Lord of the harvest to send out laborers into his harvest.'

Before we come to these verses describing Christ's compassion, Matthew has taken us upon a progression of sorts, one which culminates in our call to discipleship. Jesus begins his public ministry with the words, "Repent for the Kingdom of Heaven is near." Matthew understands we have questions about this kingdom, what is it like and what should we do? Much of his Sermon on the Mount which follows serves as our answer. "Blessed are those who are persecuted for righteousness sake, for theirs if the Kingdom of Heaven." But when Jesus comes down from the mountain, a question still lingers. Are these just words? Does this man have the power to bring about this kingdom? Can he make it so? In response Matthew presents us with a series of miracles and healings. Immediately after his sermon he heals the hand of a leper. He has the power over our infirmities. He then gets into a boat with his disciples, and when the wind threatens to capsize them, he calms the waters. Jesus possesses the power over nature.

Reaching the far shore at Gadarenes, he casts out demons who possess two men. Now we know he is more powerful than the forces of evil. In the next sequence of events, as Jesus returns home, he encounters a paralyzed man lying on his bed, but before he heals him, Jesus says his sins are forgiven. It's as if the circle is complete and our questions of power are fully answered. As the Son of God he has dominion over all things, both the physical world and the spiritual world. This kingdom will come.

It's at the end of this succession of miracles Matthew takes a step back with Jesus looking at the crowds, giving us a glimpse of how he sees us. He looks out at humanity and sees us as sheep without a shepherd, harassed and helpless. It began with the proclamation of a kingdom and a demonstration of God's power to bring it about, but now in Jesus' penetrating gaze, he's filled with a profound sense of sadness. For me no other passage of the Bible invites us to look so deeply into the mind of Christ and to see what he sees. We don't like to be called sheep, but that's who we are. We're helpless to save ourselves, unable to give ourselves the life we seek. We're harassed by a host of fears, insecurities and anxieties, often hidden so deeply within, that we hardly know our true selves. We try to compensate with masks made of egos, wealth, power and denial, but beneath those facades we're still sheep. We look for our identity in politics, gender, race and a myriad of other ways, but Jesus sees us as so much more, made in the image of God. I think his gaze is so sad because he sees us made for such heights, yet we inexplicably choose to remain in our depths. Why do we so choose when the kingdom is so near?

Matthew takes us along this progression, ending with Jesus' gaze, as our summons to discipleship. Seeing a lost world helpless and harassed, Jesus doesn't fix all the world's problems. Instead he calls for laborers. That is the essence of our vocation, to see through these eyes of Christ and to share his compassion. This Christian compassion stands in stark contrast to the world's sentimentality. Compassion sees us as more than we are and is committed to that end. Compassion will pick up a cross. Sentimentality is a light attachment to the other. In vain it tries to love in the abstract. In the end sentimentality can be distinguished from compassion because compassion is directed outward, while sentimentality is directed inward, often a pious self-image by which we morally lift ourselves above others.

Fyodor Dostoevsky captured this difference when he wrote, "The more one loves humanity, the less they love the individual." Jesus expressed a similar thought when he was asked "Who is my neighbor?" He didn't respond to the lawyer's question with a grand pronouncement that all humanity is our neighbor, although that is the case. Rather he told a story of individuals, of a Good Samaritan who stopped and helped a stranger. Our neighbor wasn't a cause without a name and a face, something distanced from us for whom we're willing to commit other people's tax dollars. Our neighbor was the person we encountered along the way, someone who needed our help.

John's Farewell Discourse not only provides us with the Spirit of Christ as this means of our becoming, which over time will be the means of our doing, but also provides our confidence. As Jesus leaves the table, he has one more thing to say, the last piece we need, "Take courage, I have conquered the world." His final words are all we really need to know. We need to remember however that it was a paradoxical statement of sorts, announcing his triumph as he was walking towards his death. Our own calling is similarly paradoxical. We're asked to go out into to an angry and hostile world and that's the world we're asked to love and serve. Like the first disciples we're asked to do what seems impossible, while the effects of what we do may never be known in our lifetime. Yet with Christ's courage and his promise of victory, we know the kingdom will come to pass. We don't deal in either pessimism or optimism concerning the future of the world. We deal in a promise. God has conquered this world. The harvest will be great, that is our certainty. All we need now are laborers.